Developing Leaders for the Church

Biblical Principles of Leadership Empowerment

Lattis R. Campbell, D.Min.

ηγεσία Press

This book may be purchased in bulk for educational use. For information, please email lattis@akmissions.us.

Cover & Interior Design: Japheth Campbell

Published in the United States by ηγεσία Press
ISBN-13: 978-0615801018

About the Author

Lattis Campbell is currently the Director of Alaska Home Missions for the Alaska Assemblies of God and is a Nationally Appointed U.S. Missionary. Along with his wife Sharlotte, Lattis has given leadership to the church as pastor, educator, missionary, and author. Lattis holds an earned Doctorate Degree in Pentecostal Leadership and a Master of Divinity in Practical Theology. He and Sharlotte served over twenty years in pastoral ministry and for the last eighteen years in education.

Before his current position, Dr. Campbell was the founding director of the Alaska School of Ministry, an ongoing educational approach that has been responsible for the leadership development and education of hundreds of men and women across Alaska.

Lattis and Sharlotte have two grown sons, a lovely daughter-in-law, and three beautiful grandchildren. At present, Lattis and Sharlotte reside in Big Lake, Alaska.

Acknowledgements and Dedication

Original Acknowledgement of Doctoral Work

The first mentor of my life, the one person who shaped my concept of God and Christianity more than any other, is my mother, Effie T. Campbell, who now awaits me in glory. My father, Johnnie V. Campbell, who taught me the life-skills of hard work, honesty, and devotion to family, still mentors me by his life. The greatest influence in my life, the one person who has stood by me, encouraged me, prayed for me, and wouldn't let me quit my educational pursuits, is my dear wife, Sharlotte. To her, I owe a debt of love and devotion.

The Doctor of Ministry experience has radically changed my life. I am not the same person as when I started the program. The Doctor of Ministry Team, the members of my cohort, and the administration, faculty, and staff of the Assemblies of God Theological Seminary deserve my heartfelt thanks and appreciation.

I am especially grateful to my project advisor and editor. Dr. Zenas Bicket and Julie Kraus were invaluable to the success of this endeavor.

The leaders of the Alaska District Council, who gave me time and space to pursue doctoral goals, and the Alaska churches, that allowed me to audition empowerment ideas and processes on them, have contributed significantly to the completion of this project and deserve God's blessings.

But, above all, to God be the glory!

Present Dedication and Acknowledgement

This book is dedicated to my wife, Sharlotte A. Campbell. Sharlotte has been the inspiring and driving influence in producing this volume of work. Without her love, commitment, and understanding, this book would never have come to fruition. Whatever I have attained in ministry, it is much more than I would have attained without Sharlotte in my life.

I also want to acknowledge the friendship, support, and editorial skill of Dr. Norman Lindsey. Norman and Judy Lindsey have been friends, supporters, and fellow-laborers through much of our journey in Alaska. If friends are part of God's blessing in life, then I have been blessed indeed because of Norman and Judy.

And, I want to acknowledge my oldest son, Japheth Campbell. Japheth's expertise and skill in book production and promotion is indeed a blessing. The successful completion of this book is due, in a large part, to Japheth's knowledge base and skill.

Contents

And the things you have heard me say in the presence of many witnesses entrust to reliable men [and women] who will also be qualified to teach others. (2 Timothy 2:2 author's revision)

About the Author..iii

Contents.. ix

Foreword..1

Introduction..3

Section 1:

Biblical/Theological Foundations of Empowerment 7

Chapter 1:

A General Definition of Empowerment and Its Biblical Context............9

Chapter 2:

Empowerment and the Genesis Account of Creation 11

Chapter 3:

The Spirit of God in the Empowerment Process 17

Chapter 4:

Old Testament Examples of Empowering Leadership Development ... 21

Chapter 5:

New Testament Examples of Empowering Leadership

Development - Jesus.. 27

Chapter 6:

New Testament Examples– The Apostles.. 35

Chapter 7:

Observations and Conclusions from Section 1 41

Section 2:

Contemporary Understanding and Ramifications of

Empowerment in the Local Church 45

Chapter 8:

Definitions of Empowerment.. 47

Chapter 9:

Empowering Culture versus Hierarchical Culture 51

Chapter 10:

Empowering and Information Sharing.. 55

Chapter 11:

Empowerment and the Creation of Autonomy Through Boundaries .. 57

Chapter 12:

Empowerment versus Delegation 59

Chapter 13:

Empowerment versus Delegation 61

Chapter 14:

Empowerment and Teams.. 63

Chapter 15:

Empowerment and Situational Leadership II® Issues 65

Chapter 16:

Empowerment and Mentoring or Coaching 67

Section 3:

Compatibility of Empowerment with Current Church

Theology and Praxis.. 71

Chapter 17:

Empowerment and the Dichotomy of Clergy and Laity 73

Chapter 18:

Empowerment and Every-Member-A-Minister 77

Chapter 19:

Empowerment and Paradigm Shift.. 83

Chapter 20:

Empowerment and The Process Church... 85

CONTENTS

Section 4:

Practical Steps toward Implementing an Empowering Culture

in the Local Church 89

Chapter 21:

Homegrown Leadership Development and

the Sharing of Knowledge... 91

Chapter 22:

The Local Church is the Seedbed for

Homegrown Leadership Development... 95

Chapter 23:

Homegrown Leadership Development as a

Product of Team Environments... 99

Chapter 24:

Homegrown Leadership Development and the Freedom to Fail......... 101

Chapter 25:

Homegrown Leadership Development and Mentoring/Coaching...... 103

Section 5:

Conclusion 105

APPENDIX A:

The Situational Leadership II® Model... 107

APPENDIX B:

Analysis of Ephesians 4:11-12 111

Bibliography 115

Foreword

There is no success without a successor.
John Maxwell

In his book, *21 Irrefutable Laws of Leadership*, John Maxwell declares, "There is no success without a successor." In other words, leaders must preserve the work they have accomplished by actively identifying and developing new leaders to assume the work once the current leaders step aside. Jesus is perhaps the best illustration of that principle. The continuation and success of the Christian Church, after the Ascension of Jesus, is due to the fact that Christ empowered those around him to assume the leadership of the ministry.

The Church of the 21st Century must emulate Christ's example of empowerment. The pages following in this book outline a process by which the Church can accomplish such a goal. These pages are the gleanings that came from my doctoral research concerning how to empower indigenous or home-grown leaders for the Alaska context of ministry. However, the biblical, theological, and practical principles described in this book are applicable to any context of ministry anywhere.

I offer this book as both a challenge and a guide. The challenge is to assume a truly biblical posture of empowerment in regard to leadership development. Unfortunately, our Adamic nature mitigates against this at times. Thus, we must pray and work to overcome those issues that hinder us, as leaders, to develop and empower other leaders.

The guide, of course, is the book itself and the definitions, steps, and resources it contains. My desire is that you read the book carefully and prayerfully and that you seek ways to implement its concepts.

Introduction

Rick Warren states, "[God] expects every Christian to use his or her gifts and talents in ministry. If we can ever awaken and unleash the massive talent, resources, creativity, and energy found in the typical local church, Christianity will explode with growth at an unprecedented rate."[1] The process of awakening and unleashing, referred to by Warren, is called empowerment. Empowerment is part of the indigenous church principle that places emphasis on developing and deploying home grown leaders for local church contexts of ministry.

The indigenous church principle, based on the example of the Apostle Paul in the New Testament, has produced strong and vibrant churches worldwide. Part of the emphasis of this principle is to develop leaders within the local culture and turn leadership over to these people. Although this seem like a simple concept on the surface, the implementation of this concept has proven challenging for many current leaders.

Those who evangelize and establish local churches often find it hard to turn loose of the leadership reigns in order to develop the potential leaders within a congregation. In 1982, Dr. A. W. Glandon, a respected educator and missionary, spoke to the issue of not adhering to an

---

1   Rick Warren, "Who's On First?: Guiding Your Members into Greater Maturity," *Enrichment: A Journal for Pentecostal Ministry* (Summer 2002): 56.

indigenous style of leadership development, "[an] adequate period of nurture is imperative but we must also recognize that an unduly extended period of paternalism and subsidy nearly always leads to immaturity and irresponsibility and eventually to resentment and resistance."[2] In light of the lack of indigenous or home-grown leaders in many churches, Glandon's words appear to be fulfilled prophecy.

Adding to the dilemma of a lack of indigenous leadership in many churches is the contribution of a hierarchal mindset of ministry, which creates a dichotomy between the clergy and the laity. This dichotomy has the inherent tendency to disempower rather than empower homegrown leaders due to its emphasis on leadership dependency.[3] In a hierarchal model of church leadership, ministry is generally viewed as the domain of the professional clergy and the laity is the recipient of ministry. An initiative to become independent from or interdependent with existing leadership is seriously lacking in a hierarchal paradigm. Historically, this hierarchal mindset of ministry has been the standard mode of organizational structure within many churches.

Because nothing happens in an organization without the active involvement of leadership, current leaders are key elements in developing and empowering future leadership. These leaders must grasp the importance of adopting and modeling an empowering leadership approach to church ministry. Additionally, because people generally only rise to the level of leadership that is expected of them and offered to them, communicating directly to everyone in the congregation concerning her or his God-

---

2   A. W. Glandon, "Far North Bible College from 'A' to Z,'" unpublished data in "A Feasibility Study on Extension Education for Theological Training Rural Alaska" by Chuck Wilson (Master thes., Oregon State University, 1990), 30.

3   Ken Blanchard, John P. Carlos, and Alan Randolph, *The 3 Keys to Empowerment: Release the Power Within People for Astonishing Results* (San Francisco: Berrett-Koehler Publishers, 1999), 250.

given abilities and capabilities for spiritual leadership is crucial to producing empowered, homegrown leaders for the ministry of the local church.

The purpose of this book, therefore, is to introduce a model of leadership development for local churches based on a theological and organizational understanding of the processes of empowerment. Empowerment will be viewed from a theological perspective with an emphasis on the Spirit's role in the empowerment process. This theological understanding of empowerment will be the focus of Section 1. An organizational understanding of the process and value of empowerment gained from a review of literature on the subject of empowerment will be the focus of Section 2. The compatibility of an empowering model of ministry within the context of the 21st Century church will be the focus of Section 3. Section 4 will deal with practical steps for establishing an empowering model of ministry within the local church. And, Section 5 will offer some conclusions to this study of empowerment.

Before beginning this in-depth look at empowerment, some key terms and concept need to be defined. Although the following key terms are fully defined within the following pages of the book, basic understandings of these key terms are given here to introduce and acquaint the reader with the terminology used for this study.

Empowerment. The basic definition of empowerment is to give power to another. This term is used throughout this book to refer to a leadership development principle in which existing leadership shares power with or releases power within followers.

Power. Power is the strength, ability, or authority to have influence in a given situation.

missio Dei. This term refers to the mission of God concerning the saving of humanity. missio Dei is the action of the Triune God in sending whatever instrument is necessary for humankind's redemption. This action involves the sending of God's Son, the sending of God's Spirit, and the sending of God's people into the world.[4]

Situational Leadership II®. The Situational Leadership II® model of leadership and leadership development describes an approach to leadership defined by the situational dynamic in which both the leader and the follower find themselves. The basic thesis of this model is that leaders must adapt their leadership style to accommodate the developmental needs of followers[5]

---

4   George W. Peters, *A Biblical Theology of Missions* (Chicago: Moody Press, 1972), 9; Lois Barrett and others, *Missional Church: A Vision for the Sending of the Church in North America*, ed. D.L. Guder (Grand Rapids: William B. Eerdmans, 1998), 5.

5   A complete description of this model of situational leadership is described in Appendix A.

Section 1:
Biblical/Theological Foundations of Empowerment

Providing a biblical foundation for the concept of empowerment is essential to our understanding of church leadership development. Although a buzzword socially, politically, and economically in the Western World, empowerment is not widely known or understood in the Christian church context. This section of the book provides a basis for understanding empowerment from a biblical theological framework.

Chapter 1

A General Definition of Empowerment and Its Biblical Context

The concept of empowerment is legitimately biblical, although the specific term is not found in Scripture. To empower, by definition, is to give power to another.[6] Understood in this definition is that before power can be given, power must be possessed. One cannot give what one does not have. Throughout Scripture, the Triune God is shown to be the holder of all power. Both Testaments of the Bible depict God as one who gives or withholds power at His discretion and will.[7]

There are several Hebrew and Greek words translated "power" in Scripture. The predominate word in the Old Testament is כֹּחַ and carries the meaning of strength or ability. כֹּחַ is basically understood as having the capacity to act.[8] In the New Testament, two words are predominate.

---

6   *Hyperdictionary* (2000), s.v. "empower," available from http://www. hyperdictionary.com /dictionary/empower; accessed 21 September 2004.

7   In the Old Testament, this concept of omnipotence (all powerful) is best understood through the various names of God and by referring to God's strength through anthropomorphic expressions such as God's arm, hand, and even finger. Additionally, passages such as Jer. 32:17, Ps. 135.6, Matt. 19:26, Luke 1:37, and Matt. 28:18 describe God as having or holding all power.

8   R. Laird Harris, ed., *Theological Wordbook of the Old Testament*, vol. 1, s.v. 973 כֹּחַ, by John N. Oswalt (Chicago: Moody Press, 1980), 436-37.

δυναμαι bears the meaning of strength or ability[9] and εξουσια carries the meaning of authority or right.[10] From these various words, "power" is understood as the strength, the ability, or the authority to exercise control or influence over a situation, environment, or person. To empower someone is to give that person the authority, ability, or strength to control or influence surrounding circumstances. As the author of Divine Empowerment, God can bestow strength, ability, and authority. As agents of human empowerment, we can only bestow authority or authorization. However, we can also empower by helping those under our influence discover or determine their God-given strengths and abilities.

Within the biblical account, God shares His power with humans. God's process of empowerment seeks to establish humankind in leadership positions with the intent of working through these leaders to empower others around them. As Edgar Elliston states, "God's plan for the spiritual empowerment of others requires the obedience and participation of existing leaders."[11] Biblical empowerment is not an end but a process and a means toward effectively equipping all the people of God to accomplish the will of God in the world.

In the following pages of this section of the book, this understanding of empowerment will be viewed from both an Old Testament and New Testament perspective. God has a purpose and design in his creation and part of that purpose and integral to that design is empowering his people for ministry and leadership in the world.

---

9   Gerhard Kittel, ed., *Theological Dictionary of the New Testament*, vol. 2, D-H, s.v. dunamai, by Walter Grundmann, trans. Geoffrey W. Bromiley, ed. (Grand Rapids: William B. Eerdmans Publishing Company, 1964), 284-317.

10   Ibid., εξουσια, by W. Foerster, 562-74.

11   Edgar J. Elliston, *Home Grown Leaders* (Pasadena, California: William Carey Library, 1992), 131-32.

Chapter 2

Empowerment and the Genesis Account of Creation

When attempting to understand anything biblical, it is always best to begin at the beginning. The work of God in this world is rooted and grounded in the creative process of Genesis. Thus, as we look for biblical paradigms of empowerment, we must begin with God's divine purpose for the world and mankind.

Empowerment Depicted in the Genesis Account of Creation

This principle of empowerment is clearly seen in the Garden of Eden when God places humans at the head of His created order and gives to Adam and Eve the care and concern of the garden and all therein. Both autonomy and accountability, necessary ingredients of empowerment, are given to the first human pair.

During this creative process depicted in the Genesis account, God empowers humankind as regents over creation. In Genesis 1:26, humans are created in order to rule over creation. The Hebrew term translated "rule"

(רדה) carries the idea of dominance or dominion. [12] Then in Genesis 1:28, this concept of "rule" is coupled together with the term "subdue" (כבש), which conveys the idea of bringing into submission by strength if necessary.[13] Thus, in Genesis 1, God empowers humankind to rule over creation by force or strength. However, proper hermeneutics forces us to interpret the events of Genesis 1 with its parallel events in Genesis 2. In this account of the creative process, man is placed in the Garden of Eden in order to cultivate or work the ground (Gen. 2:15). The term translated "cultivate" (עבד) literally means "to serve."[14] Then, "cultivate" is coupled together with the Hebrew word translated "to keep" (שמר). This term is actually a pastoral motif. [15] Man keeps or oversees God's creation by serving it through pastoral care.

Coupling the terms "serving" and "keeping" from Genesis 2 together with the terms "rule" and "subdue" from Genesis 1 indicates that humans' empowerment by God as regents over creation is to be accomplished through the attitude and heart of a servant or shepherd. This understanding of servant leadership is crucial to a proper understanding of a biblical paradigm of empowerment. To be an empowered leader in the biblical sense means to have the power to be a servant of God, willing and able through His power to accomplish His perfect will. To be empowered is not a license to be dictatorial, abusive, or mordant; rather it is a privilege given in order to be of service to the Master and to those being led.

Additionally, in this servant motif is the understanding that an empowered leader is not the final product of God's

---

12 Harris, vol. 2, s.v. 2121 רדה, by William White, 833.

13 Harris, vol. 1, s.v. 951 כבש, by John N. Oswalt, 430.

14 Harris, vol. 2, s.v. 1553 עבד, by Walter C. Kasier, 639-41.

15 Ibid., 2414 שמר, 939-40.

empowering process.[16] God empowers us in order for us to empower others. An empowering leader, one who serves God's will by equipping and empowering others, is the ultimate outcome of the empowering paradigm. Those who only seek to be empowered never fulfill the ultimate purpose of God and fall short of true servant leadership. In the words of Elliston, "Existing leaders must continue to realize that they are not the primary power holders; they are but the conduits through whom God works to empower others."[17]

God's Initial Process of Empowerment in the Genesis Account of Creation

Part of the process of man's empowerment in the Genesis account is accomplished by God's willingness to share knowledge necessary for the assignment. Man was told what he could do, what he should not do, and the consequence of disobedience. Knowledge is power, and God is willing to share adequate knowledge in order for humankind to accomplish their calling and duty.

Additionally, inherent in this Genesis empowerment motif is accountability. In the words of David Martz, "Leadership, according to the creation account, was intended to be a cooperative responsibility between God and man characterized by communication, mutual trust, dependency, and accountability to God."[18] Humans are free to exercise power within the parameters God establishes. Empowerment is not free reign. Although Adam and Eve are empowered agents of God, God establishes a boundary

---

16   In order to fulfill Gen. 1:28, Adam and Eve had to pass on the empowerment of God to their descendents.

17   Elliston, 131-32.

18   David Martz, *Leadership Development Architecture: Growing 21st Century Leaders in Cross-Cultural Bible Schools* (Springfield, Missouri: LIFE Publishers International, 2002), 18.

to their freedom. Within these parameters, humankind has total autonomy to execute power and service. Crossing over that boundary is to abuse the parameters of empowerment and incur God's punitive action. When Adam and Eve step over these parameters, they are held accountable for their actions. The first human couple, as empowered agents of God, transgresses God's authority and suffers sin's consequences. After this initial sin in Genesis chapter three, humans are still empowered, but the process becomes laborious and often times unfruitful. Only as humans yield themselves completely to God's mercy and grace can empowerment find its full potential.

One other point in this beginning motif of empowerment is that man and woman are empowered as a team.[19] Empowered teams are embryonic to the biblical account of man's creation and this dynamic carries forth throughout the rest of Scripture. Thus, there is a theology of teams that runs throughout the biblical narrative. This emphasis on team leadership finds its perfect paradigm within the Trinity and is stressed clearly throughout both Testaments of Scripture. An empowered team is the basis of God's original design for His work in the world. God-given leadership is not to be a solo act. Only as empowered teams find their full potential can the original plan of God for His creation begin to be accomplished.

The above process should be considered a divine paradigm for twenty-first century empowerment models. Emulating the creative acts of God is crucial as we seek to establish empowered and empowering leaders in the church. To withhold necessary knowledge, to fail to establish the clear boundaries of one's responsibilities, and

---

19   Gen. 1:26-28 implies that rulership was given to both sexes, not to the male alone. This team, Adam and Eve, was empowered to oversee and serve creation.

to emphasize solo leadership rather than team leadership will only result in stunting the growth of the Church.

The Purpose of Empowerment in the Genesis Account of Creation

Establishing humankind as an empowered servant-leader allows God to share the responsibility and blessings of His work in the world. This work of God is generally referred to as the *missio Dei* and designates the continuing work of God in reconciling the world to Him. Although the Triune God is the primary agent in this reconciling process, He delivers a substantial amount of the mission to people. God empowers men and women to be His agents of grace, miracles, and even judgment. Empowered people, throughout Scripture and continuing during the present age of the Church, reveal God's mission on the earth by word and deed. If the world is to be reached for Christ, the Church must continue this principle of empowerment established by God.

Chapter 3

The Spirit of God in the Empowerment Process

In the beginning stages of the Genesis account and throughout the rest of the Scriptural narrative, the ability of humankind to exercise cognitive governance and leadership is directly related to the Spirit of God. The Holy Spirit (the *ruach* of God in the Old Testament and the *pneuma* of God, its New Testament equivalent) becomes the agent by which God equips and empowers men and women to function as God's representatives in the world. Empowered leadership among the people of God is only possible through the activity of the Spirit in individual lives. The choosing of leaders, the equipping of leaders, the releasing of leaders, even the discipline of leaders, are all contingent on the influence of the Spirit in the life of the church. As Elliston states, "Spiritual leadership development is a key role of the Holy Spirit. The Spirit is the one who gives the overall supervision. He superintends, empowers, equips, gifts, guides, directs, provides insight, and delegates the authority to lead. It is *His* work."[20]

Elliston refers to this work of the Spirit as the "delegated dimension of empowerment" and is a cooperative effort

---

20   Elliston, 106.

between the Holy Spirit and existing leaders. The Holy Spirit delegates His power to emerging leaders in the form of spiritual gifts and existing leadership gives space and opportunity to allow this to happen.[21] Blanchard, Carlos, and Randolph refer to this cooperative effort, in a secular sense, as the essence of empowerment. They state, "The real essence of empowerment comes from releasing the knowledge, experience, and motivational power that is already in people but is being severely underutilized."[22] Church leaders must realize the Spirit has equipped everyone in the church with giftings and callings but much of that equipment is being underutilized due to a lack of knowledge and a lack of opportunity. Releasing this spiritual power will result in substantial church growth and ministry.

Joseph – An Example of Spirit-Empowered Leadership

An outstanding example of Spirit-empowered leadership in Genesis is the life of Joseph. This account is the first time in Scripture where the ability to lead and govern is clearly recognized as a work of the Spirit of God in a person's life (Gen. 41:37-40). Joseph's empowerment by the Spirit is clearly seen as equipping him for leadership in Egypt. Joseph's spiritual empowerment is recognized by Pharaoh, who rightly contributes it to the work of the Spirit of God, and results in Joseph's empowerment by Pharaoh to give political, social, and spiritual guidance to both the Egyptians and the Israelites.

---

21   Ibid., 124.
22   Ken Blanchard, John P. Carlos, and Alan Randolph, *The 3 Keys to Empowerment: Release the Power Within People for Astonishing Results* (San Francisco: Berrett-Koehler Publisher, 1999), 6.

Moses – An Example of
Spirit-Empowered Leadership

The episode of Moses' life recorded in Numbers 11 also serves as an example of the Spirit's involvement in the empowerment process. Implied in this narrative is the thought that Moses' ability to lead the people of God is dependent on the activity of the Spirit in his own life and that the ability of the seventy elders to lead is dependent on the same Spirit.

Only as the seventy elders are empowered by the same Spirit that rested on Moses can they give leadership to the people of God. Of particular interest in this passage is the motif of the transfer of power. God is said to have taken "of" the Spirit that was upon Moses and allowed that Spirit to rest upon the elders (Num. 11:25). However, Scripture seems to indicate this act did not diminish the spiritual power or authority of Moses. That Moses clearly understood this principle of empowerment is vividly seen in his reaction to the concern of Joshua. Joshua believes Moses' authority and influence will be diminished if others have the same capabilities as Moses, especially if they are not under Moses' direct and immediate control (Num. 11:29). However, Moses realizes as long as the seventy elders stay within the boundaries of God's covenant and execute leadership accordingly, they can be a great blessing to Israel as an empowered team of leaders. Evidently, Moses was secure enough in his relationship with God that he could allow others space and freedom to develop their Spirit-given ministries without fear of having his ministry and position undermined.

The Day of Pentecost – An Example of Spirit-Empowered Leadership

Moses' stated desire in Numbers 11 (that all of God's people would be prophets) becomes a theme that runs throughout the Old Testament and finds it ultimate fulfillment on the Day of Pentecost when the empowered servants of God become prophetic mouthpieces.[23] Spiritual empowerment becomes democratized as God pours His Spirit out on all the people of God. The prophethood of all believers, bestowed by the Spirit, equips the church to give spiritual leadership to all of humanity. Spiritual leadership is defined as moving people on to accepting God's agenda for their lives.[24] As the Church is empowered by the Spirit and speaks prophetically, the knowledge of God is revealed resulting in people accepting God's parameters for living. The Spirit then adds to the Church daily, increasing the team dynamic of empowerment. Thus, in the Church, without the involvement of the Spirit of God, empowered spiritual leadership is impossible.

---

23   Specific references to this theme are found in Num. 11:29, Isa. 59:21, Joel 2:28-9, and Acts 2:4.

24   Henry Blackaby and Richard Blackaby, *Spiritual Leadership: Moving People on to God's Agenda* (Nashville, TN: Broadman and Holman Publishers, 2001), 20.

Chapter 4

Old Testament Examples of Empowering Leadership Development

As stated previously, the process of empowerment as seen in the creative purposes of God is not just to produce empowered leaders, but empowering leaders. The Old Testament contains examples of this style of leadership development.

The Example of Moses

Not only is Moses' life emblematic of the Spirit's role in the empowering process, but the need and desire for an empowering model of leadership development is most clearly seen in his life as well, specifically in Exodus eighteen. Many modern scholars refer to this passage as a biblical paradigm of the need for the senior leader to empower others in a team effort. This chapter indicates that the traditional process of one person trying to minister to all the flock is not adequate.[25]

Moses is clearly depicted as not being able to govern or pastor the people of God by himself (Exod. 18:18). Elliston

---

25   Melvin J. Steinbron, *Can the Pastor Do It Alone?: A Model for Preparing Lay People for Lay Pastoring* (Ventura, California: Regal Books, 1987), 42.

refers to this type of leadership by the term *over-functioning leader* and defines that term as a leader who tries to do everything and decide everything.[26] Acting upon the advice of his father-in-law, and with the approval and help of God, Moses invests seventy of the elders of Israel with a measure of the authority and leadership he possesses. The selection of these elders is based on trustworthiness and honesty (Exod. 18:21). The duty of Moses as a leader is to observe these characteristics within those he leads and then to spend time imparting knowledge and modeling lifestyle to them (Exod. 18:20). Results of Moses' action are that leadership burnout will be avoided and the people of God will be fulfilled and satisfied. Melvin Steinbron believes Moses to be a prime Old Testament example of an empowering leader for the following reasons: (1) he is willing to journey with them; (2) he is willing to teach them or impart knowledge to them; (3) he selects, appoints, and trains them for responsible ministry; (4) he is there for the difficult cases; (5) he shares ministry with them; and (6) he recognizes and longs for their individual priesthood.[27]

Current leadership in the Church needs to return to its biblical roots as portrayed in this account of Moses. The problem of an over-functioning leader syndrome that presently plagues the church environment will be largely eliminated when leaders emulate the model of Moses as described above. It should be noted that in the example of Moses' empowering style, empowerment is not synonymous with abandonment. Moses stays in constant contact with his developing leaders, providing them necessary information, guidance, and backup.

---

26   Elliston, 10.
27   Melvin J. Steinbron, *The Lay Driven Church: How to Empower the People in Your Church to Share the Tasks of Ministry* (Ventura, California: Regal Books, 1997), 121-22.

Another incident in the life of Moses illustrates the empowerment process of mentoring and publicly recognizing those called to leadership. In Numbers 27, at the command of the Lord, Moses lays hands on Joshua and gives to his younger protégé some of his authority in the sight of the people of God, visually denoting to all Israel Joshua's authority and ability to lead the people of God.

Preceding this action, however, Joshua had been prepared for leadership by being with Moses in many instances of leadership training.[28] The laying on of hands is simply a public acknowledgement of the culmination of an ongoing leadership training process in the life of Joshua. However, public endorsement of emerging leaders is a necessary and crucial step in the empowerment process. Without the approval and endorsement of present leadership, emerging leaders will have an uphill struggle to gain authority and respect. A simple act of endorsement, granted to the right person at the right time, can clear the path for accelerated leadership development to transpire.

The Example of the Office of Prophet

After Israel inherited the Land of Promise, leadership became focused on the offices of prophet, priest, and king. Empowerment for the office of prophet generally came directly from God;[29] however, there are exceptions.

The relationship between Elijah and Elisha is one of the more notable of these exceptions.[30] A transfer of power from Elijah to his disciple is described in the terms of a

---

28   These instances include Exod. 17:14; Exod. 24:13ff; and Exod. 33:11.

29   A good example of this fact is the call and ministry of Amos (Amos 7:14-15).

30   The relationship between Elijah and Elisha is described in 1 Kings 1915-21 and 2 Kings 2:1-18. Although God told Elijah that Elisha was to succeed him, Elijah and Elisha shared a mentor/apprentice type relationship for some time. The transfer of power came symbolically through the sharing of Elijah's cloak with Elisha after a close relationship between the two men.

father bestowing upon his eldest son the "double portion" of blessing (2 Kings 2:9-10). Elisha became the empowered heir of Elijah's God-given prophethood (2 Kings 2:13-15). This empowerment process, though, is incumbent upon a close relationship between the mentor and the mentee. Elisha earns the right to be empowered because he is faithful to maintain an attitude of closeness and teachableness. Elijah earns the right to empower because he is faithful to maintain a position worthy of emulation.

The Example of the Office of Priest

The Old Testament priesthood in Israel is designed to be a progenitor process (Exod. 29:9). One of the sons of the High Priest is empowered to fill his father's position (Exod. 29:29-30). Implied in this process is modeling by the father and emulation by the son.[31] Due to sin, this office becomes corrupted and abused. In the economy of God, an everlasting priesthood is established in the person of Jesus Christ, who becomes the empowered, eternal Priest of the people of God.[32] Jesus, in turn, empowers His followers to priestly positions as well (1 Peter 2:5).

The Example of the Office of King

Kingship in Israel is also designed as a progenitor paradigm.[33] The throne, especially in the southern Kingdom of Judah, is passed on primarily to the eldest son with modeling and emulation as part of the process.[34]

---

31   When sons did not follow their father's example, or when the father's example was skewed, judgment came upon them from God (Lev. 10:1-3, 1 Sam. 2:27-36, 1 Sam. 4:12-21).

32   This is the basic premise of the writer to the Hebrews, especially in chapters one through ten.

33   God's promise to David in 2 Sam. 7:10-16 reveals God's intention to establish an offspring of David to sit continually on the throne of the kingdom.

34   This fact is implied by passages like 1 Kings 14:7-9, 2 Kings 14:3, and 2 Kings 15:3.

Again, however, because of sin, the throne becomes corrupt and unstable. An eternal throne and kingship is established in Jesus who is the all-powerful potentate of God's everlasting kingdom.[35] In turn, Jesus empowers men and women to serve in positions of ministry and authority within His kingdom.[36]

Team Ministry Portrayed by Offices of Prophet, Priest, and King

The offices of Prophet, Priest, and King in the Old Testament demonstrate the need for team leadership in an empowerment model of leadership development. A one-dimensional leadership paradigm is shown to be wholly inadequate to give sufficient leadership to the Old Testament people of God. These three separate offices speak to the totality of man's needs. The prophet spoke to man's need for the knowledge and wisdom of God. The priest spoke to man's need of the removal of guilt and sin. The king spoke to man's need for protection due to weakness and dependency.[37] Leadership is distributed between the three offices and each office is dependent on the other two.

Unlike other despotic kingdoms in the Ancient Near East, Israel's king was subject to the word of God as spoken by the prophet. God's word was law, not the king's.[38] The king's personal standing before God was subject to the offering of an acceptable sacrifice by the priest. The prophet and the priest held a shared responsibility for the spiritual

---

35   See Rev. 17:14, 19:16; 1 Tim. 1:17.

36   See Matt. 19:28; Rev. 1:6, 5:10.

37   R. L. Reymond, "Offices of Christ," in *Evangelical Dictionary of Theology*, ed. Walter A. Elwell (Grand Rapids: Baker Book House, 1984), 793.

38   William Sanford Lasor, David Allan Hubbard, and Frederic Wm. Bush, *Old Testament Survey: The Message, Form, and Background of the Old Testament* (Grand Rapids: William B. Eerdmans, 1982), 235.

well being of the nation.[39] God's blessing or judgment came upon the kingdom largely due to the successful interaction between these three offices.

---

39   Elmer A. Martens, *God's Design: A Focus on Old Testament Theology* (Grand Rapids: Baker Books, 1994), 156.

Chapter 5

New Testament Examples of Empowering Leadership Development - Jesus

The need for an empowering leadership development style is not diminished with the increased revelation of the New Testament writings. What began in the creative purposes of God finds its full completion in the New Testament, especially in the life and ministry of Jesus.

The Example of Jesus

As we turn to the New Testament ministry of Jesus, leadership empowerment becomes a vital part of His mission, the *missio Dei*. Although Jesus heals the sick, raises the dead, and teaches concerning the kingdom of heaven, He devotes a substantial part of His time to leadership development. Tommy Reid states, "Jesus spent far more time in ministry to His leadership team than he did with the multitudes."[40] An ongoing theme of Christ's ministry is His commitment to empower and partner together with his disciples.[41] Aaron Milavec states:

---

40 Tommy Reid, "A Spiritual Father's Reflection on Mentoring: Confessions of a Spiritual Father," *Enrichment: A Journal for Pentecostal Ministry* (Summer 1997): 48-51.

41 John H. Spurling, "Empowered Team Leaders in the Smaller Church," *Enrichment: A Journal for Pentecostal Ministry* (Fall 2001): 52-54.

No matter how supremely valid Jesus' fresh vision of God's cause might have been, if this vision was not communicated to His disciples, then it would remain exclusively His and be irretrievably lost to civilization the moment that He departed.[42]

Jesus' great commission to His church can only be fulfilled by an empowered followership. The ministry and influence of Jesus during His earthly tenure is limited to a small geographic and ethnic sphere. The worldwide spread of Christianity has to be realized by an army of disciples trained and empowered to continue the work of Jesus. Gene Wilkes says:

Jesus' ministry on earth is a striking example of an important leadership principle: Mission continues when people are captured by it, equipped to do it, and "teamed" to carry it on. When Jesus turned His motley crew of disciples into a team with a mission, He ensured that His work would continue long after He was gone... In the sense Jesus was all-powerful and could do whatever He wanted, he did not need a ministry team, but He built one so that His mission would continue when He returned to the Father.[43]

The implication from this leadership motif of Jesus is that we are not all-powerful, thus, how much more desperately should we be undertaking the empowerment

---

42   Aaron Milavec, *To Empower as Jesus Did: Acquiring Spiritual Power Through Apprenticeship*, Toronto Studies in Theology: vol. 9 (New York: The Edwin Mellen Press, 1982), 6.

43   Gene C. Wilkes, *Jesus on Leadership: Discovering the Secrets of Servant Leadership from the Life of Christ* (Wheaton, Illinois: Tyndale, 1998), 213-14.

of those we lead if we fully expect to influence the world for Christ.

In Matt. 9:35-38, Jesus gives voice to the magnitude of the *missio Dei* by expressing how large the harvest field is and how few the workers are to reap that harvest. The Lord of the Harvest then impresses upon His followers to pray that laborers will be sent and subsequently He sends forth the twelve empowered with His authority. If the Lord of the Church saw the necessity of empowering His followers in order to accomplish the mission of God, how much more should the necessity of empowerment be obvious to us? Concerning this passage of Scripture, Daniel Brown says,

> Each believer has a part to play. So significant is that part, that when Jesus comments on the harvest at hand, He urges His disciples to pray for more laborers – not for a miraculous sweep of the Spirit. For His own mysterious purposes, God has chosen to partially link His work on earth to willing human beings with whom He can form a partnership.[44]

Empowered people, not programs or institutions, are the answer to Jesus' prayer for the harvest.

Jesus' leadership training model reflects the Jewish pattern of apprenticeship and on-the-job training. This was not the only option available to Jesus. Both Jewish and Greek cultures had formal school models as an option, but Jesus chose the more non-formal mixture of dialogue, experience, and reflection contained in the apprenticeship style.[45]

---

44   Daniel A. Brown, *The Other Side of Pastoral Ministry: Using Process Leadership to Transform Your Church* (Grand Rapids: Zondervan, 1996), 118.
45   Elliston, 48-49.

This non-formal mixture involved a relational coaching approach with emphasis on an experiential on-the-job-training approach[46] based on the relationship that exists between the teacher and the student, the master and the apprentice. The goal of this style of training is enabling the learner, the apprentice, to become an empowered master or teacher who can then empower others. Jesus fully expects His followers to do as He has done, even to the point of doing it greater than He had done (John 14:12). The secret to His expectation is empowerment. John Maxwell quotes Fred A. Manske, Jr. as saying, "The greatest leader is willing to train people and develop them to the point that they eventually surpass him or her in knowledge and ability."[47] Maxwell further indicates that in order to be a great developer of people, a person must be personally secure. Developing and empowering others may take them to a height of their potential that will surpass even the potential of the developer.[48]

A relational dimension, a vocational dimension, and a spiritual dimension characterize the empowerment model of Jesus.[49] Relationally, Jesus calls His disciples to be with Him, to allow Him to mentor and empower them by His example and person. Relationship is essential in the empowerment process. Martz states, "Leading, according to biblical examples, implies a leader-follower relationship based on mutual trust, goodwill, and the principles of love, hope, and loyalty to one another and to the mission."[50] Only as the disciples walked with Christ could they begin

---

46   Tim Elmore, *Mentoring: How to Invest Your Life in Others* (Duluth, GA: EQUIP, 2001), 20.

47   John C. Maxwell, *Developing the Leaders Around You: How to Help Others Reach Their Full Potential* (Nashville: Thomas Nelson Publishers, 1995), 110.

48   Ibid., 132.

49   This statement is not to suggest there is a dichotomy that exists between the sacred and the secular.

50   Martz, 20.

to get a sense of His heart and vision. Only as they watched His example could the future leaders of the church realize the necessity of having the same power as Jesus possessed. Only as they were close enough to see Him go into Heaven and experience his absence could the apostles understand the urgency of Christ's words to wait for the promise of the Father that would empower them with Christ's continual presence.

Vocationally, Jesus empowers His disciples by entrusting to them the work and responsibility of the ministry. Jesus calls His disciples to co-partner with Him in ministry. Rarely in Scripture is the Lord found laboring in the harvest alone. He is continually demonstrating the work of God and then encouraging His disciples to do the work of God. In the difficult cases, He is always there to give advice, counsel, and encouragement.[51]

Spiritually, Jesus supernaturally empowered His disciples to carry out the work of the ministry far beyond their human capacity. Jesus would not only empower by training them and entrusting the work of the ministry to them, but He would also empower by pouring out His Spirit upon His followers. The same Spirit that equipped Jesus is promised to rest on the disciples as well.[52] And, the followers of Christ are promised even greater ministry than the Lord himself had (John14:12).

As empowerers in the Church of Christ, present leadership must follow in the footsteps of the Lord of the Church. We, too, must develop strong relationships with those we seek to empower. We must give adequate vocational opportunity to future power-brokers by

---

51   See Matt. 17:14-23 as an example of this fact.

52   This is inferred from the events of Jesus baptism in Matt. 3. The Spirit came upon Jesus, empowering him for ministry, and a baptism of the Spirit by Jesus is promised to those who accept John's baptism and witness. Also, Paul's words in Rom. 8:9-11 point to a sharing of the Spirit's power between Christ and His followers.

allowing them the privilege of working with us, ever increasing their opportunities and responsibilities, giving oversight and insight at critical junctures of the process. In addition, we must allow them to grow in the Spirit even beyond our own capabilities, praying for their success, and not being threatened when our prayers are answered.

The empowerment principle of leadership that Jesus taught is also based on an understanding that transference of power is made early in the discipleship process. Jesus began empowering people to do ministry at an early stage in His career and in the disciples' spiritual development. In the words of Wayne Corderio, "Jesus began passing the baton of leadership early in His ministry."[53] The reason Jesus could do this is because he had adequately transferred to His disciples knowledge sufficient to the tasks and had firmly established the boundaries of the Kingdom of God in which they were to function.[54] However, to keep potential power holders at bay until "perfection" is reached will not result in empowerment but in frustration and conflict.

An attitude of learning through failure is part of the empowerment paradigm established by Jesus. Jesus thrust His disciples into ministry and gave them permission to fail.[55] Jesus recognized failure as an opportunity to teach and empower. Rarely did Jesus approach his disciples' failure in a purely punitive attitude. Thus, in a very real sense, the process of empowerment is a faith-walk with potential pitfalls and failures. And, even Jesus, the Master of Empowerment, lost Judas to the process.

---

53   Wayne Cordeiro, *Doing Church as a Team* (Ventura, California: Regal Books, 2001), 113.

54   If the chronology of the Gospels is correct, it is interesting to note that the Sermon on the Mount precedes any active involvement of the disciples in ministry. The Sermon on the Mount conveyed adequate knowledge of the Kingdom of God and the parameters of that Kingdom which are two of the necessary ingredients for empowerment to take place.

55   Perhaps the greatest illustration of this fact is the denial of Jesus by Peter and Peter's restoration after Jesus' resurrection.

The empowerment model of Jesus contains two critical elements: (1) He gave His followers the authority of His name and (2) the power of His presence.[56] The disciples were empowered to cast out demons, heal the sick, and perform other miracles through the authority of Jesus' name (Mark 16:17-18). The empowerment of the name of Jesus is especially strategic in praying. God the Father recognizes and responds to the prayers of Christ's disciples when those prayers are presented in the name of Jesus (John 15:16). Although the authority of our name will not result in the same dramatic spiritual results, we can empower those we are developing with our name. By publicly endorsing those under our tutelage, we impart to them a measure of the influence associated with our name. Potential leaders must be recognized, empowered, and released to do ministry in the church. Present church leadership, in cooperation with the Spirit, is the agent to bring this about. Taking raw leadership material and forming it into positive, powerful influence for the Kingdom of God is the goal of the empowerment process. This process is laborious, time-consuming, but necessary if the Kingdom of God is to advance to the completion of the *missio Dei*. Elliston refers to this process of public acknowledgement by the term legitimation.[57] We legitimize and thus empower through granting to others whatever authority and influence our name contains.

The ultimate empowerment episode in the ministry of Jesus is the empowerment of the church on the Day of Pentecost. The very Spirit (Presence) of Jesus became resident within the lives of the disciples and the spiritual power of God permanently permeated their being. However, it must be noted that this outpouring of power only enhanced the teaching and modeling that Jesus had

---

56 Wilkes, 225.
57 Elliston, 48.

previously engaged in with His disciples. Part of the Spirit's function is to bring back those things previously heard and learned (John 14:26). The Pentecostal Baptism is not a replacement empowerment motif; rather, it is an enhancer of proper principles of empowerment. Empowered people are not created instantaneously through a unique spiritual experience. Empowered people are a product of a deliberate and often long process.

Although God is the only one capable of Spirit baptism and Spirit empowerment as evidenced on the Day of Pentecost, there is a level at which humankind can emulate this Divine empowerment motif. As humans, we cannot baptize in God's Spirit as Jesus did, but we can empower those under our influence with our own spirit or presence. Wilkes has helpful insight here:

> How does a person empower others with his or her presence? What did Jesus do? He spent time – long, deliberate time – with those who followed him. To instill the mission and its values in the team and to demonstrate their part in carrying out that mission, we must spend time with them.[58]

Our personal presence in the lives of those we are seeking to empower is critical if the process is to be successful.

---

58   Wilkes, 226.

Chapter 6

New Testament Examples of Empowering Leadership Development - The Apostles

With Christ's ascension to heaven, the task of leadership development became the responsibility of the followers of Jesus. The Great Commission carries with it the command to make disciples of those who believe. The Apostles took this command seriously and equipped for leadership those they influenced with the Gospel.

The Example of the Apostles

After Jesus' ascension and subsequent empowerment of the church on the day of Pentecost, the early church fathers, especially the Apostle Paul, emulated the empowerment motif of Jesus in developing leadership. The biblical record offers no indication that schools of ministry were developed for leadership training. Rather, the training of church leaders in the New Testament is accomplished through personal example and apprenticeships.

Throughout his New Testament writings, Paul constantly urges people to imitate or follow his example. The clearest and most succinct statement of this is found in 1 Cor. 4:16 when Paul says, "Therefore I urge you to imitate me." Modeling by personal example is an important

35

aspect of biblical empowerment. Steve Moore states that this modeling method of leadership development was a priority in Paul's life and bases his belief on Titus 2:7, "In everything set them an example by doing what is good."[59] Peter also stresses empowerment by example when he instructs the church elders to be an example to the flock of God (1 Pet. 5:3) and by the writer to the Hebrews in the instruction to imitate the faith of Christian leaders (Heb. 13:7-8).

An example of Paul's apprenticeship process is 2 Tim. 2:2. Paul's goal is to teach, train, and empower capable followers who can in turn teach, train, and empower their own followers in an ever-widening circle of influence. Biblical leadership development is based on relational mentoring models that empower home grown leaders in hands-on-ministry. This process, spiritual reproduction, is the ultimate goal of discipleship and is the leadership responsibility of every believer.[60]

It must be noted, however, that Paul's method of leadership empowerment is not a tidy and foolproof approach. A large portion of Paul's writing in the New Testament is devoted to follow-up and problem solving among those being empowered. Notwithstanding, Paul never recants his use of an empowering model even in the face of potential and actual failure. Empowerment involves great risk, but Paul appraises the reward to outweigh the danger.

The Apostle John relates much the same principles of empowerment by referring to his apprenticeship method in 1 John:1-3. In this passage the Apostle explains that his method of discipleship is based on what he himself had seen and heard, which he now passes on to others. Eddie

---

59   Steve Moore, *Leadership Insights: For Emerging Leaders and Those Investing in Them* (Fort Worth: Top Flight Leadership, 2002), 86.

60   Martz, 11.

Gibbs calls this a "contagious experience of discipleship" and indicates the early church empowered people by drawing them into the "orbit of their own experience."[61] Every believer has an orbit of experience that she or he can share with someone else; thus, every believer is to be involved in this empowerment process.

Equipped and empowered leadership roles in the early church are not just the domain of the "professional clergy." Eph. 4:11-12 indicates the responsibility and work of the apostles, prophets, evangelist, and pastor/teacher are to equip or prepare all of God's people for works of service.[62] The goal of this process is a mature people of God capable of active daily service. Empowerment is necessary to obtain this goal. Every member a minister is not a cliché, but an accurate description of the holistic approach to ministry found in the early church. Melvin Steinborn states, on the basis of Eph. 4:11-12, "Equipping lay people for ministry is God's plan for the pastoral care of His people."[63] Each person in the Body of Christ is to have the power, authority, and opportunity to actively participate in the *missio Dei*.

According to the teachings and actions of the early apostles, ministry in the New Testament church is never intended to be viewed as a "solo act." The empowerment of the entire body of Christ into a team effort is the goal of New Testament Christianity. Darrell Guder states:

> The apostolic ministry in the New Testament was carried out by teams, such as Paul, Sylvanus, and Timothy...Paul appointed groups of elders to lead the communities he founded. The Spirit is not stingy in its giftings of

---

61   Eddie Gibbs, *ChurchNext: Quantum Changes in How We Do Ministry* (Downers Grove, Illinois: InterVarsity Press, 2000), 56.

62   Please see Appendix B for a detailed analysis of this pericope of Scripture.

63   Steinbron, *Can the Pastor Do It Alone?*, 26.

the church for its mission. Every community's task is to discern those who are Christ's gift to the church as part of the apostolic-prophetic-evangelistic-pastoral-teaching Word ministry that is to equip it for its calling.[64]

Throughout the New Testament, spiritual empowerment of new leaders is demonstrated by the action of "laying on of hands."[65] This motif seems to indicate a desire to impart power and authority from elders to potential leaders in the church. Although only God can empower spiritually, prayer for and public recognition of God's approval by the eldership is demonstrated by this "laying on of hands" and recognizes those being endorsed as having spiritual power and authority. This endorsement is a vital part of the empowerment process for leadership development.

As a description of people's potential, Rom.12:6-8 speaks volumes of insight to the empowering leaders. The essence of this pericope of Scripture is the message "let him do it!" Whatever gifting a person is endowed with by the Spirit, as leaders we must step aside and let that person exercise his/her giftedness; to fail to do so results in unfulfilled spiritual potential. Paul Stevens states, "Without every-member-ministry, we have unlived biblical truths, unstrategic leadership deployment, untapped resources in the congregation, and an unreached world!"[66] Daniel Brown believes the very essence of church leadership is the act of helping each believer, in a one-on-one relationship, find and fulfill her/his God-given purpose in the church

---

64   Darrell L. Guder, *The Continuing Conversion of the Church* (Grand Rapids: William B. Eerdmans, 2000), 164.

65   See Acts 6:6, 8:17, 13:1-3; 1 Tim. 4:14.

66   R. Paul Stevens and Phil Collins, *The Equipping Pastor* (Washington, D.C.: The Alban Institute, 1993), p. XI) as quoted in Melvin J Steinbron, *The Lay Driven Church: How to Empower the People in Your Church to Share the Tasks of Ministry* (Ventura, California: Regal Books, 1997), 65.

by empowering her/him to serve "according to the proper working of each individual part" (Eph. 4:16 NASB).[67]

As indicated previously, biblical empowerment is directly correlated to the role of the Spirit of God in the lives of the people of God. The basis for Paul's argument for every member of the body being necessary (1 Cor. 12:12-26) is the equipping and empowerment of the people of God by the Spirit of God. God's Spirit equips Christ's church with a host of ministry functions that result in an empowered Body of Christ capable of adequately fulfilling the *missio Dei* in the world. To negate or hinder any member of the Body from fulfilling his/her role of ministry is to disavow the sovereign role of the Spirit in the life of the church. To believe that the Body of Christ is ill-equipped to do the work of God is a serious lack of faith in the Spirit's empowerment process. Since it is the Spirit who calls and equips for ministry, the leader of any ministry function must believe God will provide those who can be empowered for service. Wayne Corderio states:

> The first step in building a core of leaders is to believe that they are there. You must believe that God would never call a leader to oversee a ministry without providing everything necessary for its fruitfulness and success! Many pastors and ministers have the best reason in the world for why things just aren't happening like they should at their churches: "We have no leaders!" But God is not so cruel as to call you to build an ark without providing the necessary materials for its completion.[68]

Another path by which human empowerment takes place is through the avenue of prayer, public blessing,

---

67 Brown, 120.
68 Corderio, 93-94.

and standing with emerging leaders, helping to bear their burdens and tasks. Existing leaders must serve as priests. Elliston states it thus:

> Existing leaders are expected to continue from the beginning through retirement to serve as priests to intercede in prayer for the emerging leaders. They should also empower the emerging leaders through both private and public blessings. They are expected to serve as models to emulate. Existing leaders then can serve to facilitate the spiritual empowerment process by standing with/bearing with the emergent leader as he/she learns to praise, pray, meditate, fast, wait, study the word, suffer, and serve accountably.[69]

---

69   Elliston, 135.

Chapter 7

Observations and Conclusions from Section 1

Although God is the ultimate source and repository of all power and is thus the ultimate empowering person, humankind also has an active role in the empowerment process. Ultimately, it is the Spirit that calls, guides, and equips but God uses men and women in the process. The sharing of power by one leader with others is demonstrated by the Old Testament examples of Moses and the seventy elders and Elijah and Elisha. The development of ministry teams is demonstrated by these same examples and is also portrayed by the three-fold leadership paradigm of prophet, priest, and king in the Old Testament. In the New Testament, Jesus empowers His followers with the authority of his name and with the power of His presence.[70] The apostles emulate the paradigm of Christ's empowering process in the lives of their own disciples.

Stephen Macchia indicates that just as Jesus made extraordinary leaders out of ordinary people, so we too, under the guidance of Jesus' Spirit, should be empowering potential leaders by giving them opportunity to flourish and utilize their gifting and talents, especially in the areas where we are not strong. Macchia states forcefully, "We

---

70   Wilkes, 225.

dare not hold others back from the potential that is within them, planted there by God himself."[71] Although we cannot empower people with our presence in the way Christ does (through the indwelling Spirit of Christ), we can empower people with our presence in the sense of being willing to spend time with them, publicly recognize them, pray for them, and be there to encourage and support them. Additionally, we can help them to find their giftings and callings, emphasizing to them that ministry is not the sole domain of the professional clergy. Infusing them with this knowledge alone can result in substantial leadership development.

Helping those under our influence to establish the boundaries of their ministry potential is also important. Because empowerment comes through understanding clearly divine boundaries, helping people establish biblical boundaries of mission, values, and vision results in empowerment. A clear understanding and acceptance of these boundaries free both the one empowering and the one being empowered. The empowerer can grant autonomy and the freedom to fail, knowing that those under his or her tutelage will not overstep the clearly established parameters of the church. The empowered can exercise freedom and autonomy without fear of unclear expectations or punishment.

The empowerment paradigm is not without potential danger, however. Jesus lost Judas to the process and Paul spent large amounts of time and energy in following-up and problem solving. But neither Jesus nor Paul discount the necessity of the process.

The ultimate goal of the empowerment process is to produce a team-based effort toward helping fulfill the *missio Dei*. God equips each person with unique callings

71   Stephen A. Macchia, *Becoming A Healthy Church: 10 Characteristics* (Grand Rapids: Baker Books, 1999), 130.

and gifts. Existing leaders must place great emphasis on blending each person's potential into the overall mosaic of God's work on earth. Ministry must no longer be defined or portrayed as belonging solely to the professional clergy. This middle-wall of partition must be abolished, allowing all of God's people to exercise their God-given giftings and callings. Just as Moses prayed that all of God's people would become prophets, we must pray that all of God's people will find their places of leadership within their spheres of influence. Steinbron states:

> The differences between laity and clergy are not in order, but in function. Peter's definition of the Church – a "royal priesthood" – establishes the fact that only one order exists. That one order is priest (or minister); however, God has given it many functions.[72]

Existing church leaders must view this challenge of empowering and mobilizing every member of the church as a crucial mandate, not an option. Sue Mallory and Brad Smith state, "Gift-based service is not an optional activity, but the activity for which we were created."[73] This empowerment process will result in the Body of Christ being built up, attaining the unity of faith and the knowledge of God's Son, and becoming mature and reaching the fullness of the measure of Christ.[74]

---

72   Steinbron, *The Lay Driven Church*, 51.
73   Sue Mallory and Brad Smith, *The Equipping Church Guidebook* (Grand Rapids: Zondervan, 2001), 31.
74   Author's paraphrase of Eph. 4:12.

Section 2:

CONTEMPORAY UNDERSTANDING AND RAMIFICATIONS OF EMPOWERMENT IN THE LOCAL CHURCH

It is evident from Section 1 of this book that empowerment is a necessary ingredient of the leadership development process by which God seeks to accomplish the *missio Dei* in the world. We must ask, however, do our current church leadership development processes include empowerment as a dynamic element? Specifically, are we empowering a broad spectrum of the church for effective spiritual leadership in the world? And, if such processes are implemented, will that result in an increase in indigenous church leadership? To answer these questions, Section 2 will review contemporary research on leadership empowerment and apply the results to the church's context of ministry.

This review will focus on:

(1) contemporary definitions and understandings of empowerment,

(2) the compatibility of legitimate empowerment with current church theology and praxis,

(3) and the relationship between empowerment and the development of indigenous or home-grown church leadership.

Chapter 8
Definitions of Empowerment

Much has been written in current literature concerning empowerment and its application to organizational success. A summary of contemporary definitions and understandings of the empowerment process reveal how empowerment can play a crucial role in leadership development.

Definitions of Empowerment

Although the simple definition of empowerment is giving power to another, a more expanded understanding of empowerment reveals the depth and complexity of the process. Leadership empowerment is actually releasing the power that is already resident in each individual. Ken Blanchard, John Carlos, and Alan Randolph write, "Empowerment is not giving people power...People already have plenty of power – in the wealth of their knowledge and motivation...We define empowerment as letting this power out."[75] Blanchard, Carlos, and Randolph also write, "The real essence of empowerment comes from releasing the knowledge, experience, and motivational power that

---

75   Ken Blanchard, John P. Carlos, and Alan Randolph, *Empowerment Takes More Than a Minute* (New York: MJF Books, 1996), 13.

is already in people but is being severely underutilized."[76] According to these definitions, empowerment takes place when leaders recognize and release followers' abilities, talents, and passions. Gary McIntosh states:

> Empowerment is an active term giving authority and responsibility from one in charge to a subordinate. Empowerment in the church takes place when pastors and church leaders delegate responsibility for ministry to laypeople and actually allow them to do ministry. It means that pastors and church leaders allow laypeople to participate or act on the power they already have through the Holy Spirit.[77]

The acknowledgement that followers already possess power is crucial to the empowerment process and is in complete alignment with the biblical teaching of omnipotence belonging to God. The power that leadership gives in the empowerment process is the permission and authority to act on the spiritual and natural power resident in each follower through God's enabling. This transfer of power (permission to act) is clearly demonstrated when leadership removes bureaucratic boundaries which inhibit effective use of skills, experiences, energies, and ambitions; allows a sense of ownership to develop for areas in which people are specifically responsible; and demands that people act responsibly by accepting ownership of the larger organizational effort.[78]

---

76   Ken Blanchard, John P. Carlos, and Alan Randolph, *The 3 Keys to Empowerment: Release the Power Within People for Astonishing Results* (San Francisco: Berrett-Koehler Publishers, 1999), 6.

77   Gary L. McIntosh, "Empowering a New Culture of Service in Your Church," *Enrichment: A Journal for Pentecostal Ministry* (Fall 1998): 37.

78   Warren Bennis and Michael Meshe, *The 21st Century Organization* (San Francisco: Jossey-Bass Publications, 1995), 36.

In the church context, empowerment is the desire and ability of the pastor to give ministry up so that lay people can be developed to the place where they see themselves as viable ministers in the Kingdom of God.[79] Blanchard asked organizational leaders what they wanted from their employees and vice versa. The leaders replied, "We want people who are problem solvers, who take initiative, and who act like they own the business."[80] Translated into church terminology these leaders would be saying, "We want church members who sense the burden and needs around them, who take responsibility to meet those needs, and who behave like the church and its mission is their duty." The employees replied:

> We want honesty. Tell us the truth about how our company is doing; we can handle it and we can help improve the situation. In addition, we want to learn new skills that will not only help us here but we can take with us if we have to look for another job.[81]

Translated into church terminology these followers would be saying, "Pastor, be straightforward. Challenge us with genuine needs - we want to help. But, we need you to equip us, to show us how our gifts and talents can be used in the kingdom." Leaders want empowered people and people want to be empowered. However, both leaders and people generally do not know how to go about the process.

Although speaking of mobilization, Daniel Brown actually defines empowerment by saying, "Mobilization means recruiting the right person for the job, equipping

---

79   Kristi Rector, "Power to the People – How Pastors can Empower their Congregations to be Lay Pastors: An Interview with Melvin Steinbron," *Vital Ministry: Innovative and Practical Ideas for Pastors* (July/August 1998): 44-45.

80   Blanchard, *3 Keys*, 5.

81   Ibid.

that person for the task, and releasing him or her to serve in meaningful ways."[82] Richard Dresselhaus refers to the principle, "A good leader will work himself or herself out of a job," as the essence of empowerment. Effective leaders train and model so that others can step in and do the job efficiently.[83] David McKenna adamantly states that the essence of effective leadership can only be determined after the leader leaves and the followers build upon the base of the former leader.[84] At the heart of an empowering style of leadership development is the unselfish desire to equip, promote, and release each person in the organization to perform at the maximum of his or her ability. Empowerment is giving people permission to become engaged in a meaningful way[85] and allowing them to act responsibly.

---

82   Daniel A. Brown, *The Other Side of Pastoral Ministry: Using Process Leadership to Transform Your Church* (Grand Rapids: Zondervan, 1996), 133.

83   Richard L. Dresselhaus, "The Long Reach of Laity," *Enrichment: A Journal for Pentecostal Ministry* (Fall 1998): 57.

84   David L. McKenna, *Power to Follow, Grace to Lead: Strategy for the Future of Christian Leadership* (Dallas: Word Publishing. 1989), 172-73.

85   McIntosh, 37.

Chapter 9

Empowering Culture versus Hierarchical Culture

Changing to a permission-granting or empowering environment is a major shift for hierarchal-based institutions such as the traditional church. Eddie Gibbs writes:

> To move...to a permission-giving leadership and management style requires significant adjustments. Controllers operate from a premise of distrust and suspicion. They build dependency networks around themselves, which bolster their egos and ensure their position by making them indispensable...Controllers tend to be insecure people who surround themselves with "clones" or individuals of lesser ability who will pose no threat...Permission givers are ambitious for the people working around them and are not intimidated by people more able than themselves. Permission givers are in the business of growing people, not of "cloning" people.[86]

---

86   Eddie Gibbs, *ChurchNext: Quantum Changes in How We Do Ministry* (Downers Grove, Illinois: InterVarsity Press, 2000), 85-86.

Giving people permission to try, experiment, and even fail is a truly empowering style of leadership[87] and will result in the dynamic growth of both leader and follower.

Becoming a permission-granting organization involves great risk, but reciprocally it contains great reward. Empowering people by granting permission means that leadership allows creativity and entrepreneurship that may result in ideas and processes contrary to the way senior leadership would approach a situation. For leaders steeped in hierarchal tradition, such a divergence from strict control poses a great threat. Anarchy and disrespect for the vision of leadership could ensue. However, there are great rewards associated with this type of empowerment process. Bobbie Reed and John Westfall describe the benefits of becoming a permission-granting organization. They speak to it in the terms of relinquishing control:

> The benefits to relinquishing control are several. The body of Christ is strengthened as more of the individual members are empowered to go forth and minister to one another and the world. Individual people have multiple opportunities to grow and to develop new skills and ministries. You are free to see the big picture of the total ministry rather than getting a distorted perception because you are too close to the details. And the creative ideas, the ministry and outreach, grow exponentially as more and more people get involved.[88]

Creating a culture of empowerment necessitates great change for both leaders and followers.[89] Margaret Wheatley comments, "Those who have led their organizations into

---

87   Bobbie Reed and John Westfall, *Building Strong People: How to Lead Effectively* (Grand Rapids: Baker Books, 1997), 135-138.

88   Ibid., 189.

89   Blanchard, *3 Keys*, 16.

new ways of organizing often say that the most important change was what occurred in themselves."[90] To move an organization toward a culture of empowerment requires leadership to accept new ideologies, new roles, and a new emphasis on teamwork. In an empowering culture, command and control is no longer the focus of leadership. Wheatley states, "Most of us were raised in a culture that told us that the way to manage for excellence was to tell people exactly what they had to do and then make sure they did it."[91] In an empowering culture, rather than directing, controlling, or supervising people, leadership serves more as a coordinator or coach, making sure people have the resources and networking needed to accomplish the mission of the organization, thereby enabling people to be more effective. The leader actually begins working for those he or she is leading, rather than their working for the leader.[92] A servant leader mentality is essential for an empowering culture. According to Howard Young, "The test for Christian servant leadership is the progressive spiritual health, freedom and autonomy of those served."[93]

Trust is also a crucial element leaders must develop in an empowering culture. Those who are in a controlling motif of leadership operate from a premise of mistrust. This mistrust demonstrates itself in not being able to allow people to do things differently than the leader would do them, or in not allowing people the opportunity to fail. Controllers are more concerned with performance or the bottom-line (is the task being completed) than with people's personal development. Personal development,

---

90   Margaret Wheatley, "Goodbye, Command and Control" *Leader to Leader,* No. 5 Summer 1997; available from http://drucker.org/leaderbooks/ L2L/summer97/wheatley.html; accessed 6 October 2004.

91   Ibid.

92   Blanchard, *More Than a Minute,* 23.

93   Howard Young, "Rediscovering Servant Leadership," *Enrichment: A Journal for Pentecostal Ministry* (Spring 2002): 34.

however, is an integral part of the empowerment process. Neil Eskelin likens the process of empowerment to the action of stretching out in a hammock. All of the leader's weight and faith is put on something that he or she is convinced will not fail or let down.[94] As leaders demonstrate this trust, empowerment and acceptance of responsibility among followers take place as a direct result.

Expecting people to accept responsibility is a major shift for those accustomed to a non-empowering culture. In a hierarchal culture, there is a strong dependence on leadership and an equally strong desire to place responsibility on someone else. In an empowering culture, people move away from solely depending on others for leadership to a condition of independence from, or interdependence with, leadership,[95] resulting in having to accept responsibility for their actions. In the words of Blanchard:

> Empowerment is not just a culture of involving people in the company. It is also a culture of holding people much more accountable for bottom-line results as well as the actions and development of people than is ever the case in a hierarchical culture...[96]

If approached and facilitated properly, an empowering culture generates great rewards, in spite of the increase in personal responsibility. These rewards include a sense of ownership; the satisfaction of being listened to and understood; and making use of and further developing one's talents.[97]

---

94   Neil, Eskelin, *Leading with Love: and Getting More Results* (Grand Rapids: Fleming H. Revell, 2001), 85.

95   Blanchard, *3 Keys*, 250.

96   Ibid., 190.

97   Ibid., 201.

Chapter 10

Empowering and Information Sharing

The beginning of the journey toward an empowering culture within an organization is marked by a conscious decision by senior leadership to share the wealth of knowledge they possess. Blanchard observed, "If a leader is willing to share the power that information represents, people hear – more clearly than any words can express – that this leader is reducing the barriers and including people into the circle of influence and involvement."[98] Unfortunately, many leaders hesitate to take this initial step toward an empowering culture of leadership development. This hesitancy is often based on apprehensions concerning trust and relinquishment of control. Can the common person be trusted to act responsibly on insider information? Will sharing insider information result in a loss of control over the direction and future of the organization? In other words, what will happen if present leadership relinquishes its power to fully command and control the institution, ensure its course, and guard its reputation? However, these concerns can be mediated by understanding how information sharing affects empowerment.

Information sharing has the capacity to begin empowering people immediately. Brown states that the

---

98   Ibid., 48.

easiest way to empower someone is to share information and authority (the right to act on that information) with the person. People are empowered when they receive information which they understand is not known to just everyone.[99] As people receive this power in the form of information or knowledge, they are then compelled to act on it. Blanchard affirms,

> People without information cannot make good business decisions, nor are they motivated to risk making decisions in such a void. On the other hand, people with information are almost compelled to take the risk of making business decisions to the best of their abilities.[100]

Along with the information, however, people must be given a viable opportunity to put the information to work. In the words of Brown, "Hands-on implementation is equally important as information in the empowerment process."[101] However, implementing hands-on involvement may require additional knowledge in the form of training and coaching. Sharing information is a continual process if people are to be truly empowered in any organization.

99   Brown, 134.
100   Blanchard, *3 Keys*, 48.
101   Brown, 135.

Chapter 11
Empowerment and the Creation of Autonomy Through Boundaries

Some leaders fear the loss of control and direction that information sharing may foster within an empowering culture of leadership development. Instituting the concept of "autonomy through boundaries" minimizes this fear of anarchy and disregard for the vision of the organization.[102] Empowerment is not consistent with allowing people to act selfishly or irresponsibly. Rather, empowerment is the process of helping people act synergistically by surrounding them with common mission, vision, and values and then allowing them to act unencumbered within those boundaries. A primary job of leadership in an empowering culture is to successfully transmit and instill sufficient knowledge within followers concerning the legitimate boundaries of acceptable organizational behavior. In this regard, one author believes the biblical phrase for empowerment is "stimulating one another to love and good deeds,"[103] which describes the broad biblical parameters encompassing the work of the church. However, leadership must sharply define these parameters as to the

---

102 Blanchard, *More Than a Minute*, 40.
103 Brown, 122.

specific values, goals, and processes that characterize each local congregation's involvement with the *missio Dei.*

The type of information to be shared must be commensurate with the focus and task of the person to be empowered. As the empowerment process progresses, information sharing will need to be amended and enhanced to cover the increased demands of the person's development, needs, and desires. As already stated, information sharing is a continuous need within the process of empowerment.

Chapter 12

Empowerment versus Delegation

Empowerment must not be confused with simple delegation. Empowerment is not merely delegating work and responsibility to subordinates in order to release the leader from his or her workload. Melvin Steinbron gives insight into the differences between delegating and relinquishing (his word for empowerment) responsibility to others. Steinbron states, "...don't confuse delegation with relinquishment. When you delegate, you retain ownership, expecting the person to do the work 'as it ought to be done'...Relinquishing frees; delegating freezes..."[104] Carl George echoes Steinbron's sentiment by stating, "The watchword of the future is not to 'delegate,' in the sense of handing work off to someone else, but to 'share the ministry.'"[105] Distinguishing between delegation and empowerment is crucial to the empowering process. Delegation implies that the follower is being privileged to help the leader's job be accomplished. Empowerment implies that the leader is helping the follower find and accomplish her or his own responsibility and function in the *missio Dei*. George indicates the essence of the

---

104   Melvin J. Steinbron, *The Lay Driven Church: How to Empower the People in Your Church to Share the Tasks of Ministry* (Ventura, California: Regal Books, 1997), 133.

105   Carl F. George, *The Coming Church Revolution: Empowering Leaders for the Future* (Grand Rapids: Fleming H. Revell, 1994), 64.

difference between empowering and delegating when he says that the goal is not to save time for clergy or create a mentality of "helping" the pastor. Rather the idea is apprenticeship development that says "I am sharing the privilege of doing ministry with you, because you, with supervision and training, can be just as capable a minister, if not more so, than I am."[106]

When mere delegation takes place instead of empowerment, performance rather than development is the outcome and the basis of evaluation for the follower. Brown encapsulates this sentiment by saying,

> Giving people tasks in church in order to empower them is a completely different mind-set from giving people tasks to get performance out of them. Delegating jobs with performance uppermost in mind actually frustrates empowerment. (They either fail or succeed – if they fail, we blame them and never delegate to them again; if they succeed we lock them in and never give them opportunity to go beyond).[107]

However, if people are empowered with development as the goal, failure is seen as teachable moments and successes are seen as stepping-stones to greater achievements. In the words of Brown, "The real work of ministry is not getting the work done; it is using the work to get people done."[108] And getting people done is the true focus of empowerment.

---

106 Ibid., 45.
107 Brown, 126.
108 Ibid.

Chapter 13

Empowerment and the Permission to Fail

Leaders must give people permission to fail if leadership development is to succeed. This permission involves the leader resisting the temptation to meddle in or micromanage the process of the task given to the follower. Henry and Richard Blackaby state, "Nothing will demoralize staff faster than leaders who constantly meddle in their work. Once a task has been assigned to someone, it needs to belong to that person."[109] Again they state,

> At times it is better to sacrifice perfection if doing so will develop leaders in the process. Leaders must regularly resist the temptation to interfere in their people's work. Leaders whose people are reluctant to work for them or leaders who experience difficulty recruiting volunteers should consider whether this is because they have developed a reputation for meddling.[110]

When failure happens on the part of a developing leader, senior leadership must frame the failure positively by viewing failure as an opportunity for learning to take

---

109 Henry Blackaby and Richard Blackaby, *Spiritual Leadership: Moving People on to God's Agenda* (Nashville: Broadman and Holman Publishers, 2001), 137.

110 Ibid., 138.

place. Additionally, failure may be viewed as a result of trying a new or innovative idea and not merely a reason for punishing a mistake.[111] Failure can result from improper training methods, lack of information or instruction, mismatching of skills with the assignment, or a deficiency in the person performing the work.[112] All of these potential causes must be considered. In other words, failure must not be used solely as an occasion to assess personal blame but to assess methodology. If the methodology is at fault, fix it. If the person is at fault, either through a mismatching of skills with assignment or through some personal deficiency, encourage him or her and work with the person to overcome the problem if possible.

---

111   Blanchard, *3 Keys*, 70.

112   John C. Maxwell, *Developing the Leaders Around You: How to Help Others Reach Their Full Potential* (Nashville: Thomas Nelson Publishers, 1995), 108.

Chapter 14

Empowerment and Teams

An empowering model of leadership development places great importance on the concept and function of teams. Whereas hierarchies are built around individual responsibility, empowering organizations are built around team efforts.[113] Replacing hierarchical structures with self-directed teams is one of the three keys listed by Blanchard for creating an empowering culture in an organization.[114] Although the initial objective of empowerment is to release individual ability and accountability, to fully maximize an individual's potential requires teamwork. Teamwork provides a necessary safety net as individuals are learning to function in an empowered way. Additionally, it is within teams that individuals learn the relational processes needed to successfully accomplish the mission and vision of the organization. As Brian McLaren says, "Leadership happens through teams of people being who they are and doing what they are gifted to do."[115] Stated another way, leadership in an empowering organization becomes diffused and multiplied through the deployment of self-directed teams. Since "empowerment comes from teaching others things they can do to become less dependent on you,"[116] the leader, it is incumbent on those being

---

113   Blanchard, *3 Keys*, 162.
114   Blanchard, *MoreThan a Minute*, 59.
115   Brian D. McLaren, *The Church on the Other Side: Doing Ministry in the Postmodern Matrix* (Grand Rapids: Zondervan, 2000), 113.
116   Blanchard, *More Than a Minute*, 64.

empowered to learn to depend on one another's gifts, talents, and abilities. The best place for this to happen is in a team-based environment. Additionally, team learning, so essential for the success of the organization, is achieved. Team learning happens as team members challenge each other's assumptions.[117] Such learning is necessary in order to meet the complex challenges of an organization, challenges for which no one single individual has the answers.[118]

Self-directed teams of gifted individuals are the ultimate outcome of the empowering process. When this outcome is beginning to be achieved in an organization, leadership becomes a possession of the entire organization, not just a few individuals at the top. If leadership is understood as giving direction and support to a group of people, then in an empowering culture it is the individuals within teams that both direct and support each other and the organization as a whole.[119]

---

117   Jim Herrington, Mike Bonem, and James H. Furr, *Leading Congregational Change: A Practical Guide to the Transformational Journey* (San Francisco: Jossey-Bass, 2000), 140.

118   Ibid., 130.

119   Blanchard, *3 Keys*, 16.

Chapter 15

Empowerment and Situational Leadership II® Issues

The journey toward empowerment within an organization is contingent upon the interaction between leaders' skills and styles and followers' aptitude and development. This interaction has been best described and explained by using the leadership development model known as the situational approach. This approach, detailed by Blanchard in the Situational Leadership II® model,[120] has as its basic premise the fact that different situations demand different kinds of leadership and that followers' competence and commitment levels require varying degrees of direction and support from leaders.[121] Because empowerment is a new concept to many, requiring the acquisition of new skills, new knowledge, and new commitment levels, senior leadership must adapt its style to compensate for the needs of developing leaders.

As the journey toward empowerment commences, there is an excitement or high-level of commitment toward the prospect of being empowered. Correspondingly, however, there is a general lack of understanding of the

---

120   See Appendix A for a detailed description of this model.
121   Peter G. Northouse, *Leadership: Theory and Practice,* 2ᵈ ed. (Thousand Oaks: Sage Publications, 2001), 55-56.

steps needed to implement the process. Leadership, at this point, must adopt a high directive, low supportive style of leadership behavior. Developing leaders must be given crucial information concerning what is expected of them and how to begin accomplishing those expectations. Since morale or excitement is high, very little support in the form of motivation or encouragement is needed.

Once the process has commenced and people begin to see what is required of them in order to accomplish empowerment, enthusiasm begins to wane. Leadership must adopt a high directive, high supportive style of leadership in order to continue giving direction to the developing leaders while at the same time helping them overcome their waning enthusiasm.

As developing leaders become skilled and knowledgeable, and as their successes breed renewed confidence, senior leaders must then adopt a low directive, high supportive style of leadership. This style allows developing leaders to build on their expertise and confidence, allowing senior leadership to begin stepping into the background, acting as cheerleaders for the progress of the team.

The final stage of development for empowerment is achieved when senior leaders can adopt a low directive, low supportive style of leadership which indicates developing leaders have reached an empowered level of development and are free to operate independently within the parameters of the mission, vision, and values of the organization.[122]

---

122 These incremental steps are my synopsis of Blanchard, *3 Keys*, 19-43.

Chapter 16

Empowerment and Mentoring or Coaching

The process described in the situational leadership model is best accomplished through the practice of mentoring or coaching. John Spurling writes:

> The movement in ministry focus from a narrow to a broad-based team leadership model will call for certain adjustments in the leadership style of the pastor. At the heart of this leader shift is the need to focus less on *telling* and *doing* and more on *coaching* and *mentoring*. Pastoral leadership within an empowered-team model seeks to inspire and influence leaders and potential leaders within the church.[123]

Inspiring and influencing best takes place within a mentoring or coaching relationship.

Mentoring has been described as a relational experience in which one person empowers another person through sharing God-given resources.[124] These resources are often intangible, being in the form of knowledge, guidance, and encouragement. Mentoring has also been

---

123   John H. Spurling, "Empowering Team Leaders in the Smaller Church," *Enrichment: A Journal for Pentecostal Ministry* (Fall 2001): 54.

124   Tim Elmore, *Mentoring: How to Invest Your Life in Others* (Duluth, GA: EQUIP, 2001), 16.

described as "...a brain to pick, a shoulder to cry on, and a kick in the seat of the pants."[125] Relationship is the key within this process. Mentoring or coaching[126] cannot be done at a distance or in short, infrequent spurts of effort. The stronger the relationship exists between the mentor/coach and the mentee/team, the more empowerment that takes place.[127] This empowerment is referred to as the "power to grow"[128] and continually leads to greater plateaus of empowerment.

Mentoring leads to empowerment because within the mentoring experience people develop or discover their potential for ministry[129] and are afforded the opportunity to apply that potential within a safe environment. There is immediate feedback and help if difficulty or failure is experienced. Rather than being stymied due to lack of success, failure is reframed as an opportunity to learn and progress. Additionally, there is immediate praise and encouragement when success is achieved.

Empowerment through mentoring or coaching is the way servant leaders prepare and produce the next generation of leaders. Servant leadership is not achieved until a ministry team has been built so that the *missio Dei* can be accomplished. [130] It is important to point out, in this context, that empowerment through mentoring transcends the first generation of leadership development. Anyone who has a talent or gift that has been discovered, developed, and employed can in turn mentor someone else. Mentoring or coaching is an every-widening

---

125 Ibid., 17.

126 Coaching involves much of the same dynamics as mentoring. Rather than done with an individual, coaching is done more with a team.

127 Elmore, 88.

128 Ibid., 24.

129 Ibid., 16.

130 C. Gene Wilkes, *Jesus on Leadership: Discovering the Secrets of Servant Leadership from the Life of Christ* (Wheaton, Illinois: Tyndale House Publishers, 1998), 236.

empowerment principle of leadership development. In addition, mentoring does not need to wait until an organization has grown to any specific size or maturity level. In an article by Rick Knoth, Jim Wideman says:

> In any size church, modeling, mentoring, and duplicating your heart into somebody else is the key. If you are by yourself in a small church and take just one other leader and duplicate yourself in that person, you have doubled the effectiveness of your ministry.[131]

The process of mentoring, however, must have a conclusion. Although empowerment is a product of the mentoring relationship, if the mentee is not finally released to do ministry on his or her own, disempowerment will result.[132] Gibbs states:

> Church leaders must learn that people need to be released to use their God-given gifts in response to a God-given calling. The task of the leader is to serve in a mentoring relationship of mutual accountability so that discernment may be exercised to identify the true motivation of the person being mentored while providing wise counsel and spiritual support. But people must be free to make their decisions and to carry the responsibility for the course of action to which they commit themselves.[133]

---

131 Rick Knoth, "Children's Ministries – Building Tomorrow's Church: Interview with David Boyd, Dick Gruber, and Jim Wideman," *Enrichment: A Journal for Pentecostal Ministry* (Summer 2001): 10.

132 Reed, 134.

133 Gibbs, 70.

The task of the mentor is accomplished when the mentee can do the job as efficiently, or even more efficiently, than the teacher.

Section 3:

Compatibility of Empowerment with Current Church Theology and Praxis

Within the church, many might ask if the above leadership development paradigm is preferable or even possible. As one church leader stated,

> ...Christian leaders are tentative. They want to empower people, but not that much. They are concerned that people won't lead... the way they were trained or that they won't stay faithful to the vision of the pastor. They're afraid that someone might decide things are better another way, teaching ideas contrary to the pastor and leading them to leave the church. Training, expectations, loyalty, strict rules – these ideas are the ministry modus operandi for much of the leadership in the body of Christ. They often express themselves through systems that ensure that the people ministering in the church do it as the leadership would do it.[134]

---

134 Ted Haggard, *Dog Training, Fly Fishing, & Sharing Christ in the 21st Century: Empowering Your Church to Build Community Through Shared Interests* (Nashville: Thomas Nelson Publishers, 2002), 72.

The attitude of "not granting that much power" to the people sitting on the pews of modern churches is a natural reaction for those trained in a hierarchal mindset of ministry leadership. Churches functioning within a paradigm of hierarchy maintain that ministry and spiritual leadership is the domain of the professional clergy.

So, the question becomes, "Will it work? Will empowerment result in leadership development within the local church in a way that is positive and sustainable?" The following pages are offered as evidence that the answer to this question is in the affirmative.

Chapter 17

Empowerment and the Dichotomy of Clergy and Laity

Modern church models generally incorporate a sharp dichotomy between "ministers" and "lay people." Steinbron states:

> The office of pastor is considered by most people to be the highest position in the Church. This notion, however common, is an unfortunate development because it has forged a dichotomy, creating two classes of Christians: laity and clergy...The origin of this error is traced to the fourth century when the church adopted the hierarchical structure of the Roman Empire, instead of staying with the New Testament "body" model.[135]

Seventeen centuries later, we are still embracing a model that places spiritual and ministerial power in the hands of a select few, rather than diffusing that power throughout the whole of the church body. Stanley Ott writes:

> We have taught a generation of churchgoers that ministry is either "what the minister does"

135 Steinbron, 49.

or leading as a church officer and participating in church programs...But it means that only about 20 percent of the typical congregation "have a ministry" at any given time, and the other 80 percent are on the sidelines.[136]

Traditionally, within modern denominations, great value is placed on the call and the function of vocational ministers.[137] Generally speaking, vocational ministers see themselves as occupying one or more of the five-fold ministry gits given to the church: apostle, prophet, evangelist, pastor, or teacher (Eph. 4:11). The local church looks to one or more of these offices (usually occupied by the pastor or his hired staff) for the majority of ministry-functions. Ministry is seen as existing primarily in the realm of the clergy with laity helping by filling lesser offices and performing tasks that are more mundane. This dichotomy results in the laity allowing the professional clergy to perform the "work of the ministry." Thus, ministry becomes the domain of the professional clergy.

Training for the role of "chief ministry provider" is the focus of many Bible colleges and seminaries. Bill Easum states, "Equipping is a fundamental change for professional clergy. Most have been trained to enable and to perform ministry for the congregation."[138] Steinbron refers to one minister who said he had to totally unlearn much of what his seminary experience had taught him.[139] Professional church leadership is primarily taught how to do ministry, not how to develop ministers. With this

---

136 Stanley E. Ott, *Twelve Dynamic Shifts for Transforming Your Church* (Grand Rapids: William B. Eerdmans, 2002), 80.

137 "Vocational minister" refers to credentialed ministers within the movement who generally have the responsibility of full-time service to the church and receive their livelihood from the church.

138 Sue Mallory and Brad Smith, *The Equipping Church Guidebook* (Grand Rapids: Zondervan, 2001), 49.

139 Steinbron, 31.

mindset, ministry is performed *toward* the laity rather than *with* the laity and the laity adopts a consumer mindset that militates against the need for widespread empowerment of the body of Christ.

Consumerism among the laity stands opposite to the principle of "Body Ministry" as described in the New Testament. Instead of the Body functioning together to accomplish a specific task or goal, much of the Body is lethargic and inactive. Because spiritual leadership is seen as the sole domain of the professional clergy, the laity exists to supplement the vision and function of the professional minister. A dependency model begins to exist among the regular members of the church, resulting in a climate of disempowerment. Leadership for the church is generally sought outside of the local environment and only those local people with outstanding qualities and/or personalities are considered for leadership development.

Chapter 18

Empowerment and Every-Member-A-Minister

The results of the disempowering model of leadership previously described are revealed in the words of Paul Stevens, "Without every-member-ministry, we have unlived biblical truths, unstrategic leadership deployment, untapped resources in the congregation, and an unreached world!"[140] The untapped potential that exists in local congregations needs to be utilized by establishing an empowering model of leadership development. Robert Slocum strongly states, "The most important decision facing [the] church today is the decision to shift the focus of [the] church from the ministry of the clergy to the ministry of the laity."[141]

This empowering of the laity for ministry is being referred to as a new Reformation. In the reformation of Luther's day, the Word was given back to the people, resulting in an understanding of the priesthood of all believers. This new Reformation centers on the ministry being given back to the people, resulting in an

---

140   R. Paul Stevens and Phil Collins, *The Equipping Pastor* (Washington, D.C.: The Alban Institute, 1993), XI.

141   Robert E. Slocum, *Maximize Your Ministry* (Colorado Springs: NavPress, 1990), 170.

understanding of the servanthood[142] of all believers. Steinbron states in this regard:

> In the first Reformation, the Church gave the Bible to the people. In the second Reformation, the Church is giving the ministry to the people. The Church is again becoming a classless Church. The disparity of laity and clergy is being replaced by the parity of all the people of God (the *laos*).[143]

Only one class exists in the church, servants of Jesus Christ. Within that one class are different functions of ministry or servanthood, but servanthood is available and incumbent on all of the Body of Christ.

A primary means of establishing an empowering culture is to deal with the every-member-a-minister concept. The sharing of this knowledge, and the active modeling of its implications, will begin moving a church toward indigenous leadership development by setting people free to serve responsibly within a team-ministry environment. Empowering churches help each person realize his or her gifting and calling for ministry and hold them responsible to be good stewards. These churches put an emphasis on each person being equally important in ministry. The only difference lies in function.[144]

Attempting to negate or simply ignoring the necessity for empowering all of the Body of Christ for active ministry is a serious issue, resulting in robbing the people

---

142   The term "servant" and "servanthood" adequately translate the New Testament concepts of minister and ministry. The NT uses about three or four words for minister or ministry, however, all of these words have the understanding of one who is a servant or laborer. The most common word for minister in the NT is the word **diakonos**. It literally means to wait on tables and is a description of the most common type of slave in a great household.

143   Steinbron, 50.

144   Ibid., 23.

of their God-given tasks and giftedness.[145] Equipping and empowering people for ministry is the bottom-line of what leadership should be doing in the church.

Ephesians 4:11-12 is best described as the mission statement for church leaders.[146] The purpose of the fivefold ministry given to the church is not to do all the work of the ministry but to equip the people of God to do the work of the ministry.

The utilization of the potential power within the people of God must be the primary focus of church leadership, according to Ephesians 4:11-12. The retiring bishop of a large denomination offered this reason why his branch of the church was losing membership, "...there must be a total re-emphasis on empowering the laity."[147] This underutilization of the laity is a primary reason that the *missio Dei* is not being fully realized in the world and the reason there is a dearth of leadership in the 21st Century church. According to the Barna Research Group, only 23% of all churches have any type of lay leadership team in place,[148] which would seem to indicate that 77% of all churches are doing an inadequate job of developing lay leaders.

Michael Slaughter suggests it is the utilization of the "unpaid servant" that will determine the success or failure of the mission of Christ.[149] The "laity" of the church is the most plentiful and abundant leadership resource

---

145 George Cladis, *Leading the Team-Based Church: How Pastors and Church Staffs Can Grow Together Into a Powerful Fellowship of Leaders* (San Francisco: Jossey-Bass Publishers, 1999), 15.

146 Mallory, 14.

147 Norman Shawchuck and Roger Heuser, *Leading the Congregation: Caring for Yourself While Serving the People* (Nashville: Abingdon Press, 1993), 166.

148 Sidebar, *Enrichment: A Journal for Pentecostal Ministry* (Spring 2002): 62.

149 Michael Slaughter, *UnLearning Church* (Loveland, Colorado: Group Publishing, 2000), 152.

available,[150] yet the lack of trained leaders is the most limiting factor in most churches.[151] To develop the pool of potential leaders, churches must look inward as well as outward. George Barna states, "One of the most impressive and important elements of leadership in highly effective churches is that most of the leadership comes from the laity."[152] Churches that are experiencing vitality and life have developed processes to give the ministry back to the laity to the extent that the church's philosophy states that laity should be the primary ministering people in the church.[153] Carl George states, "It's the multiplying of lay ministers, not the hiring of more church staff, that holds the key to the advance and expansion of the church in the next generation."[154]

One caveat to the above process must be noted. Gibbs cautions:

> Churches committed to developing their own leadership must also recognize the limitations of the "in-house" apprenticeship training approach. This can result in a narrow vision and in producing leaders who only know how to do what is already being done.[155]

These limitations can be guarded against by allowing outside influence to positively affect the church's training methodologies and by encouraging those being trained to participate in higher education involvements. Additionally, it will be necessary at times to hire someone from outside the local environment to enhance the church's ministry

---

150 George, 42.

151 Ibid., 41.

152 George Barna, "Nine Habits of Healthy and Highly Effective Churches," *Enrichment: A Journal for Pentecostal Ministry* (Summer 2002): 70.

153 Steinbron, 23.

154 George, 47.

155 Gibbs, 87.

efforts. However, the fear of these limitations should not be used as an excuse to preclude the necessity of empowering the laity in the local church.

Chapter 19

Empowerment and Paradigm Shift

A move toward an empowering model of leadership development that places emphasis on equipping the entire body of Christ will be a radical change for most churches. A major paradigm shift must take place in the attitude and understanding of professional clergy as well as in the mindset of those categorized as laity. However, the necessity for this change is rooted in the authority of Scripture. Empowering the entire body of Christ is not a radical departure from Scripture; it is a necessary return to a New Testament model of the church. But because this ideology is foreign to many church leaders and followers, it requires a total reprogramming of thought and action.

Professional clergy must be willing to step aside and allow gift-based ministry to begin happening among the laity. Clergy must give freedom and authority for this to transpire. The professional clergy must view laypeople as authentic ministers, equal in importance to the clergy.[156] Pastors must believe and demonstrate that those working as laypersons in the church are just as much ministers as those who preach from the pulpit.[157] This seismic shift in understanding is described by Steinbron when he says:

---

156 Steinbron, 38.
157 Clancy P. Hayes, "Training: The Secret of Pastoral Success," *Enrichment: A Journal for Pentecostal Ministry* (Fall 2002): 61.

If pastors seek clients to deliver to, they're really in the traditional mode. But if pastors can change so they see people as partners in ministry – people to whom God has given gifts to carry on ministry – then pastors can see their own roles as totally different.[158]

Clergy must share adequately and passionately the knowledge that laity are ministers in their own right and must model this knowledge with appropriate behavior.

Once the concept of every-member-a-minister is embraced, taught, and modeled, it will have great empowering potential.

Blanchard points out that only when leadership is willing to share power do people actually hear what the leader is saying about including them in the circle of influence of the organization.[159]

158 Rector, 44.
159 Blanchard, *3 Keys*, 48.

Chapter 20

Empowerment and The Process Church

Developing people to achieve their fullest potential is part of the process of transformational[160] or empowering leadership.[161] Brown refers to this type of developmental approach as becoming a process church and states, "When we see church as a process of touching people and transforming them, it shifts our focus away from the programs, the building sites for those programs, and the staff needed to maintain those buildings and programs."[162] Instead, the focus is on the process of developing, equipping, and releasing people into ministry. Brown lists several advantages to becoming a process or empowering-based church verses a program-based church. These benefits are listed in table 1.

Becoming a process-oriented church will dramatically reduce the ever-present need for quality personnel that exists in many churches. Brown believes that in reality there is not a lack of willing volunteers in most churches but a lack of thought and training. He maintains that people can become qualified to do ministry if they are

---

160 Although transformational leadership goes beyond the scope of this project, part of the process of being a transformational leader is empowering people.

161 Northouse, 136.

162 Brown, 21.

Table 1. Comparison of Program-Based and Process-Based Churches

Program-Based Church	Process-Based Church
Fear of loss or negative impact on program due to personal failure	Forgiving system that views failure as part of the process of learning
Focus on performing	Focus on training
Availability and quality of programs increase with larger size and budget	Process can begin with any size, any budget
Focus on finding talented personnel to run programs	Focus on training all workers for service
Result of growth is large number of dependent people needing ministry	Result of growth is large number of mature, fruitful disciples doing ministry

Source: Daniel A. Brown, *The Other Side of Pastoral Ministry: Using Process Leadership to Transform Your Church* (Grand Rapids: Zondervan, 1996), 28-32.

given time and teaching.[163] This process-orientation must be intentional and proactive. Empowerment will not transpire by happenchance or default. Blanchard writes, "Too many leaders think that if they and their people want empowerment, it will 'just naturally happen.' Nothing could be further from the truth."[164] The job of present church leadership must become focused on pathways of discipleship that are intentional and personalized in order to meet the individual needs, gifting, and callings of each person in the church.[165]

As a church takes on an empowering motif of leadership development, the role of senior leadership must be viewed differently than the role of senior leadership in a traditional, hierarchal model. One does not lose her

---

163 Ibid., 125.
164 Blanchard, *3 Keys*, 8.
165 Slaughter, 41.

or his job or influence by accepting an empowering role; one's role simply changes.[166] Instead of viewing itself as the primary ministry giver, the professional clergy must adopt a role of equipping and supporting others in their ministry efforts. Instead of being the sole repository of spiritual guidance and direction, the clergy must release the ministry gifts resident in the body of Christ. According to Bobbie Reed and John Westfall:

> One of the roles of ministry is providing spiritual direction. It must be kept in mind, however, that not all of that role is necessarily filled by the pastor or staff members. People within the body who are released to minister will be channels of spiritual direction from the Holy Spirit. When we retain all of this role for ourselves, we set ourselves up as spiritual gurus to whom everyone must come and from whom everyone must get their spiritual nourishment. That is not only draining on us but also restricts God's work in our ministry. He can work through all of our people, not just through a designated pastor.[167]

The difference in roles between professional clergy and lay leaders is illustrated in table 2. In this chart, Steinbron refers to professional clergy as vocational pastors and lay leaders as volunteer pastors. This graph points to the great need for professional clergy to create a culture where volunteerism is valued and upheld.[168] Volunteerism is highly valued when every member is considered a minister and is equipped to pursue ministry. When the role of both

---

166 Blanchard, *More Than a Minute*, 23.

167 Reed, 76.

168 Bill Hybels, "The Y Factor: In Tough Times, You Need to Radically Increase Your Ministry's Volunteer Quotient," *Leadership: A Practical Journal for Church Leaders* 24, no. 1 (winter 2003): 78.

laity and professional clergy is clearly understood and the laity is released to adequately fulfill its role, the institutional strength of the congregation is increased. When reliance is solely placed on the professional clergy as the primary strength of ministry, the congregation is much more vulnerable to not adequately fulfilling its calling.[169]

This process of equipping all in the body of Christ results in a very practical outcome for the church. As each person in the church assumes her or his role, under the guidance of the Spirit and empowered by both the Spirit and the senior leadership, a perpetual model of ministry development is created. Everyone becomes equipped and responsible to empower others in an ever-widening circle of influence.

Vocational Pastors	Volunteer Pastors
Overall care	Grassroots care
Care of all members	One-on-one care
Nurture, mobilize, equip	Basic congregational care
Emergency, short-term care	Ongoing pastoral care
Care of the whole church	"One anothering" (1 Thess. 5:11)
Crisis and special needs care	Regular care
The larger matters	Hands-on care
General care	Frontline care

Table 2. Difference in Roles of Vocational and Volunteer Pastors

Source: Rector, Kristi. "Power to the People – How Pastors can Empower their Congregations to be Lay Pastors: An Inteview with Melvin Steinbron." *Vital Ministry: Innovative and Practical Ideas for Pastors* (July/August 1998): 44.

---

169 Lyle E. Schaller, *The Small Church is Different!* (Nashville: Abingdon Press, 1982), 134-35.

Section 4:

Practical Steps Toward Implementing an Empowering Culture in the Local Church

Although it is clear from the previous discussion that empowerment is a necessary ingredient in the life of the church in order to facilitate the *missio Dei*, what is the relationship between empowerment and the development of indigenous or homegrown church leaders? In other words, is there sufficient data to warrant that empowerment will lead to the development of homegrown leaders? And, if so, what does such an empowerment model of homegrown leadership actually look like?

The chapters in this section are short but hopefully very practical. In addition, they are not exhaustive in example, but hopefully provide enough example to be illustrative.

Chapter 21

Homegrown Leadership Development and the Sharing of Knowledge

Empowerment happens when leaders teach people things they can do to become less dependent on the leaders.[170] As people become less dependent, they assume leadership for those areas themselves, accepting responsibility for the success or failure of the enterprise. Melvin Hodges refers to this acceptance of a sense of responsibility within developing Christians as the "pearl of great price" which results in indigenous (homegrown) leadership.[171] This principle of indigenous leadership development has worked well in mission settings around the world, resulting in strong national leadership for those contexts of ministry.

According to John Maxwell, new leaders are created and inspired when existing leaders show faith in their followers and help them to develop and hone leadership skills and abilities they didn't know they possessed.[172] It should be obvious that if potential leaders are unaware of the skills and abilities they possess, they will not be inclined

---

170   Blanchard, *More Than a Minute*, 64.

171   Melvin J. Hodges, *The Indigenous Church: A Complete Handbook on How to Grow Young Churches* (Springfield, MO: Gospel Publishing House, 1976), 17.

172   Maxwell, 11.

to seek leadership development on their own. Gibbs postulates there are two critical elements in successful leadership training: identifying the potential leader's self-identity (who the person is in God) and identifying and developing the potential leader's gifts.[173] If existing leaders do their part in observing, inspiring, identifying, and challenging potential leaders among local church congregants, homegrown leadership will be created, inspired, and developed.

The very fact that leadership can be learned and is available to all[174] is knowledge that can liberate those who have been trained in a dependency model and can inspire them toward pursuing leadership development. Empowerment has the capacity to instill three necessary but missing ingredients in the lives of those who have been subjected to paternal[175] influences: self-worth, security, and competence. When these necessary ingredients are restored to a life, the potential for leadership development is enormous. Once people see themselves as potential ministers they are motivated and willing to serve.[176]

Because every Christian is in effect already a leader with the ability to influence those around him or her in a positive way, it can be stated that everyone has a natural ability to be a minister for God.[177] When people are told that this type of ministry or leadership is not rocket science, but anyone can do it who has an open heart to the Spirit of God and who is willing to be discipled, [178] leadership development naturally ensues.

---

173 Gibbs, 106-108.

174 Northouse, 11.

175 "Paternal" refers to treating indigenous people very much like children, making them dependent on the senior leadership due to their perceived lack of maturity and/or ability.

176 Rector, 45.

177 Haggard, 15.

178 Ibid., 155.

The job incumbent on the local church is to share this knowledge clearly, succinctly, and repetitively. Furthermore, this knowledge sharing must be accompanied by an equipping culture in which laity is instructed in finding their ministry gifting and then given meaningful opportunity to use that gifting in relevant and significant ministry venues.

One excellent way to share this knowledge and to help equip all believers for ministry is through gift discover and ministry aptitude tests. Such tests are available through various channels, however, a good source and tool has been developed by the author of this book. Copies of this material are available upon request or by visiting the author's website.[179]

---

179 http://lattis-sharlotte.org/downloads/cat_view/6-leadership-development-tools

Chapter 22

The Local Church is the Seed Bed for Homegrown Leadership Development

E dgar Elliston posits:

> Local churches provide the primary arenas for identifying, selecting, and developing the whole range of Christian leaders... What happens in the local church precedes, compliments, supplements, and legitimizes what happens in Christian higher education.[180]

The development of homegrown leaders, if Elliston's proposition is correct, must begin at the local church level. To begin at the higher education level, the process most often adopted in Western churches and on foreign mission fields overseen by Westerners, will result in only those who can adapt their lifestyle to such a process being trained for leadership. However, developing an adult learning mentality that trains and empowers beginning at the local church level will facilitate a broader participation in indigenous leadership training.

Robert Clinton believes that a major function of existing leaders is the selection of rising leadership. Clinton defines the word "selection" as:

---

180   Elliston, 4.

...observing who God is selecting and processing and finding ways to enhance their development. Awareness of processing concepts can mean that you can much more efficiently advise and mentor emerging leaders. You can point them to informal and non-formal training which you know can move them along in several of the developmental patterns.[181]

The only way for this selection and developmental process to work effectively is to observe potential leaders in their natural habitat, the local church. It is in the local church setting that God demonstrates His calling and equipping of future leaders.

It is estimated that only 10 percent of American church members are active in any type of ministry while 40 percent of American church members have expressed an interest in ministry but have never been asked or have not been trained.[182] The lack of ministry participation among the laity may well be a direct result of the fact that we have not because we ask not. Part of the job of present leadership is to help everyone understand that meaningful ministry is available to all.

Meaningful ministry must be understood in the context of empowerment. Slocum correctly states that ministry must not be viewed as getting laypersons involved in the ministry of the church but getting the church involved in the ministry of the laity.[183] Gibbs explains Slocum's statement by saying:

---

181 J. Robert Clinton, *Leadership Emergence Theory: A Self-Study Manual for Analyzing the Development of a Christian Leader* (Altadena, CA: Dr. Bobby Clinton, 1989), 21.

182 Rick Warren, "Who's On First?: Guiding Your Members into Greater Maturity," *Enrichment: A Journal for Pentecostal Ministry* (Summer 2002): 56.

183 Slocum, 170.

"...church professionals represent 2 percent of church membership, and a further 18 percent consists of the "church laity," who are needed to assist in running the church's ministries...[but] what about the remaining 80 percent "worldly laity?" Slocum argues that the task of the 20 percent should be to provide resources for the 80 percent for their ministry in the world.[184]

If, indeed, we can equip and mobilize this 80 percent of unutilized or underutilized indigenous church members, spiritual leadership will occur as they assume and facilitate the calling of God in their lives.

---

184   Gibbs, 88.

Chapter 23

Homegrown Leadership Development as a Product of Team Environments

Leadership takes place when people operate as teams, being themselves and doing what they are gifted to do.[185] George Cladis states:

> The most effective churches today are the ones that are developing team-based leadership. This pattern will likely continue into the twenty-first century, both because Scripture emphasizes Spirit-led, Spirit-gifted, collaborative team fellowship and because today's culture is receptive to such leadership.[186]

Empowering laypeople by helping them discover how they can team together and work with the professional clergy will result in active leadership development. Team ministry flattens hierarchies and helps conceptualize the truth that there is no such thing as a passive Christian; all are to be involved in ministry. The mission of the Church

---

185 McLaren, 113.
186 Cladis, 1.

becomes widely shared and available to all.[187] Leadership development among the laity is the natural product of team ministry.

If at all possible, a pastor or ministry leaders should never do ministry alone. When ministry opportunities arise, the leader should allow those whose gifting meshes with the opportunity to do ministry alongside the leader. Becoming a supporter and facilitator of the ministry of the laity should become the focal point of the clergy.

Team ministry in the local church ensures that ministry and leadership is shared and does not become the sole domain of the professional clergy. Team ministry also enables the influence of the local church to go far beyond influence of a single individual or a paid professional staff. And, team ministry guards against the cessation of ministry efforts when changes occur within the professional ministry staff. Even though the professional staff person leaves, the team can continue to function.

Perhaps the greatest illustration of the effectiveness of teams is the model that Jesus used during his earthly ministry. The team Jesus developed continued after his departure and the team's ministry resulted in the worldwide effectiveness of the church that reaches even to this hour.

---

187 Cladis, 15.

Chapter 24

Homegrown Leadership Development and the Freedom to Fail

Giving people freedom to fail, one of the necessary ingredients of empowerment, and then helping people to learn from those failures without punitive action will help facilitate indigenous believers' trust in the empowerment process and will speak loudly to them concerning their ability to be innovative leaders. Making mistakes and learning from them is the pathway to empowerment.[188] Only when we give people the freedom to fail do we also give them the freedom to succeed.[189] Sharing this view of failure with those in the pew, many of whom in the past have been trained to depend on the professional clergy for leadership and have not been trusted with leadership themselves, will result in empowerment in their lives and will result in leadership development.

Because of the high moral standard that we in the church hold to, giving people freedom to fail is not the default response when it comes to empowering people for ministry. The typical action when someone fails at a task is to set them aside. Although not meant, perhaps, to be

---

188 Blanchard, *3 Keys*, 71.
189 Reed, 68.

punitive, this action results in people being disempowered and disenfranchised. Meaningful ministry is withheld from such a person until "faithfulness" and "trustworthiness" can be determined. This generally results in long stretches of inactivity and even insecurity for those so set aside

A much more biblical and empowering model is that of Jesus and Peter after Peter's denial of Christ prior to the crucifixion. Rather than setting Peter aside, Jesus understood the ministry potential that Peter possessed and was not willing to let a failure stand in the way of Peter's ultimate fulfillment. Peter's powerful sermon on the Day of Pentecost was a direct result of the Spirit's empowerment. But, the very fact that Peter was present on the Day of Pentecost was a direct result of Jesus' empowering model of leadership development that included the permission to fail and to learn from that failure.

Our churches will have its share of Peters. The potential development and leadership capabilities of these Peters will depend on how leadership in the church treats failure and recovery from failure.

Chapter 25

Homegrown Leadership Development and Mentoring/Coaching

The process of indigenous or homegrown leadership development is best done within an environment of mentoring or coaching. The relationship that exists within a one-on-one mentoring experience is best suited for the greatest potential of development and is very accommodating to cultures that place great value on relationships. The process of seeing something done, rather than merely hearing how it is done, breeds confidence. The art of doing a task with someone as a guide develops ability. The satisfaction of successfully accomplishing a mission and having a tutor give evaluation, positive criticism, and praise is very empowering. Elmore states, "Humans 'own' truth much more quickly when it is learned from relationship and experience [rather] than from a sterile classroom."[190]

Mentoring has the capacity to continue the empowering process to the next generation of indigenous leadership. Anyone can be a mentor. All that is necessary is that a person has learned something from God and is willing

---

190 Elmore, 21.

to spend time with and pass that learning on to someone else.[191] Indigenous people mentoring and empowering other indigenous people is the ultimate goal of homegrown leadership development.

Present leadership in the local church must begin this process of mentoring/coaching by personal example. Leaders must be willing to share their knowledge, their expertise, and their time, thereby demonstrating to potential leaders both the value of mentoring/coaching and the potential of such a model.

Once again, Jesus becomes the great paradigm of this process. It is no accident that the disciples were recognized as having been with Jesus (Acts 4:13) because their ministry emulated that of their Master mentor and coach.

---

191 Ibid., 17.

Section 5:

Conclusion

This survey of *Developing Leaders for the Local Church* speaks to three very specific facts. First, empowerment is a clearly demonstrated method for utilizing the potential power that lies largely dormant in the followers of most organizations. This process of empowerment is accomplished by knowledge sharing, creating boundaries for autonomous behavior, building a culture in which failure is reframed as opportunities, deploying teams as the primary means of leadership, and adhering to a process of mentoring or coaching.

Second, although empowerment is clearly the biblical approach to leadership development and is organizationally functional, current church models are more disempowering due to a dichotomy existing between clergy and laity. This false dichotomy will be abolished when every member of the church is viewed as a legitimate minister and when every believer is allowed to pursue service to God based on the equipping of the Holy Spirit.

Third, an empowering paradigm of ministry will result in an increase of indigenous church leadership. Ministry models around the world speak to this fact and the processes of empowerment ensure its outcome.

Appendix A:

THE SITUATIONAL LEADERSHIP II® MODEL

A three-dimensional management theory first introduced by W. J. Reddin is the basis for the situational leadership theory and approach. Its focus is on leadership in situations and implies that different leadership skills must be employed in different types of leadership situations. In this model, leadership is composed of both directive and supportive types of behavior; a leader must apply each of these types, or some combination of types, toward those he is leading, depending on the followers' competence and commitment to the task. As the followers' competence and commitment levels change, the leader must change styles in order to continue leading effectively. The goal of the situational leadership approach is to move followers from a developing stage to a developed stage, thus allowing leadership to go from an initial directing style to a more empowering leadership style.

Blanchard, Zigarmi, and Zigarmi have made this view of leadership popular with their Situational Leadership II® model. This model refers to the four styles or behaviors that leadership must incorporate in order to move followers along in their developmental stage. The developmental stages of followers' behavior flow from needing high support to low support from the leader. Leaders give directive behavior in the form of one-way communication clarifying what is to be done, how it is to be done, and who is to do it.[192] Leaders also supply supportive behavior in the form of two-way communication that gives social and emotional support to others. This type of behavior involves asking for input, helping with problem solving, giving praise, sharing information, and listening.[193] The goal of the model is to move followers from a stage of initial development to a stage of being fully developed.

Situational Leadership II® describes four styles of leadership that a leader must assume in order to lead followers through their developmental stages and these four styles correspond to the four stages followers' progress through on their journey to development. The first style of leadership, called S1, is a highly directive style with low supporting behavior. This style is used with followers who have very low skills or competence for the job at hand. It is assumed these followers will be highly motivated to accomplish a new task but lack the skills or competence to do so. The second style, S2, is also a highly directive style, but involves high supportive action as well. This style corresponds to followers who are growing in skills but are now less motivated due to the novelty of the situation having waned or due to difficulty with the task. Style S3 involves high supportive behavior but less directive behavior from the leader. Need for this style of leadership corresponds to the need of followers who have gained some successes with their new tasks and are also growing in confidence. The last style, S4, is a low supportive, low directive style of leadership and corresponds to followers who have become extremely developed in their skills and competence and are highly motivated to continue and accomplish their tasks.

---

192 Ibid., 57
193 Ibid.

One of the strengths of the situational leadership model is that it is prescriptive rather than merely descriptive in value.[194] When used in a real-life environment, an evaluator can prescribe certain actions on the leader's part that need to take place due to the development level of the followers. When attempting to move toward an empowering culture within an organization such as a church, a consultant can help senior leadership understand how their styles of leadership must change as followers are moved toward empowerment. Followers can be helped to understand the process of development and the various stages they will face as they progress toward becoming empowered.

---

194   Ibid., 60.

Appendix B:

Analysis of Ephesians 4:11-12

Although there is little confusion about the correct way of interpreting verse eleven of this text, there are various ways interpreters have connected the three phrases found in verse twelve: "for the perfecting of the saints, for the work of the ministry, for the edifying of the body of Christ(KJV)." Depending on the translation, one can understand that God gave the gifts of leadership in verse eleven in order to do the work of the ministry, or to equip the saints to do the work of the ministry. The question of how to interpret this passage hinges on whether the three phrases in verse twelve are independent of each other or if the latter two are dependent on the first.[195]

If one translates this passage with independent phrases, then those in leadership positions (apostles, prophets, evangelists, pastors, and teachers) are given to perform the work of the ministry that will in some way work together with the saints being perfected and the body of Christ being edified. Ministry, in this interpretation, becomes the sole domain of the leadership in the church. In addition, edifying the body becomes the sole domain of the leadership as well.

However, the meaning changes when the passage is translated with the last two clauses being dependent on

---

195 Francis Foulkes, *The Epistle of Paul to the Ephesians: An Introduction and Commentary*, Tyndale New Testament Commentaries (Grand Rapids: William B. Eerdmans, 1963), 120.

the first. This translation results in leadership in the church being given to perfect or equip the saints so that they in turn can do the work of the ministry so the body of Christ can be built up. Ministry, in this scheme of interpretation, becomes the domain of everyone in the church. R. Lenski states,

> The thought is this: to every one of us as the saints who form the *Una Sancta* Christ gave some as apostles, some as prophets, etc., for the purpose of providing the necessary equipment for all to engage in the blessed task of ministering to each other so as to upbuild his body, the church itself.[196]

The author of this book accepts the view that the duty of leaders is to equip the saints so that the saints can do the work of the ministry. It is interesting to note that the word Paul uses in Eph 4:12 which the KJV translates as "perfecting" is the Greek word καταρτισμος. Elsewhere in the New Testament this word is used for the mending of nets (Matt. 4:21) or for the restoration of the lapsed (Gal. 6:1). It can also be applied in a surgical sense to the setting of a broken bone.[197] Gerhard Delling speaks of this word in the sense of equipment for the saints.[198] This word seems to speak to the fact that the purpose of leadership is to mend, restore, and generally equip the saints in order

---

196   R.C.H. Lenski, *The Interpretation of St. Paul's Epistles to the Galatians, to the Ephesians, and to the Philippians* (Minneapolis, MN: Augsburg Publishing House, 1937),531.

197   Frank E. Gaebelein, ed. *The Expositor's Bible Commentary: with the New International Version of the Holy Bible, vol. 11, Ephesians – Philemon*, by A. Skevington Wood (Grand Rapids: Zondervan, 1978), 58.

198   Gerhard Kittel, ed., *Theological Dictionary of the New Testament*, vol. 1, A-Γ, s.v. καταρτισμος, by Gerhard Delling, trans. Geoffrey W. Bromiley, ed. (Grand Rapids: William B. Eerdmans, 1964), 475-76.

for the saints to function in ministerial capacities so that the body of Christ can be built.

Bibliography

Alaska Ministry and Cultural Issues

Corral, Roy. *Alaska Native Ways: What the Elders Have Taught Us.* Portland: Graphic Arts Center Publishing, 2002.

Glandon, A. W. "Far North Bible College from 'A' to Z.'" Unpublished data in "A Feasibility Study on Extension Education for Theological Training Rural Alaska" by Chuck Wilson. Master thes., Oregon State University, 1990.

Miller, Ralph. "An Examination of the Work of the Assemblies of God in Alaska." D.Min. diss., International Bible Institute and Seminary, 1985.

"Saint Herman Theological Seminary 2003-2004 Catalogue." Available from http://www.alaskanchurch.org/shs/pdf/Catalog0304.pdf. Accessed 5 February 2005.

Smith, Craig Stephen. *Whiteman's Gospel: A Native American Examines the Christian Church and Its Ministry among Native Americans.* Manitoba: Indian Life Books, 1997.

Supplemental Resources – Talking Circles. Available from http://www.saskschools.ca/~aboriginal_res/ supplem.htm. Accessed 8 December 2004.

University of Alaska Anchorage Publications. "VI. Organizations and Programs to Improve Alaska Native Employment." Available from http://www. iser.uaa.alaska.edu/publications/client/afnjobs/ intchvi.pdf. Accessed 22 December 2004.

U.S. Census. Geographic Comparison Tables – American FactFinder Web site. Available from http://factfinder.census.gov/servlet/GCTTable ?_bm=y&-geo_id=04000US02&-ds_ name=DEC_2000_PL_U&-_caller=geoselect&-_ lang=en&-redoLog=false&-format=ST-7&- mt_ name=DEC_2000_PL_U_GCTPL_ST7. Accessed 14 December 2004.

Wilson, Chuck. "A Feasibility Study on Extension Education for Theological Training Rural Alaska." Master thes., Oregon State University, 1990.

Wilson, B. P. *The Assemblies of God in Alaska.* Anchorage: Alaska District Council, 1980.

Empowerment and Leadership Development

Bandy, Thomas G. *Coaching Change: Breaking Down Resistance, Building Up Hope.* Nashville: Abingdon Press, 2000.

Barna, George. "Nine Habits of Healthy and Highly Effective Churches." *Enrichment: A Journal for Pentecostal Ministry* (Summer 2002): 70.

Barrow, Ed. "Creating a Competitive Human Capital Advantage." National Association of Workforce Boards, March 4, 2002. Available from http://www.nawb.org/html/2002forum/town-Barlow.pdf. Accessed 5 February 2005.

Bennis, Warren and Michael Meshe. *The 21st Century Organization.* San Francisco: Jossey-Bass Publications, 1995.

Betzer, C. Dan. "From Pew to Pulpit – Preparing Laity for Full-Time Ministry." *Enrichment: A Journal for Pentecostal Ministry* (Winter 2003): 78-83.

Blackaby, Henry, and Richard Blackaby. *Spiritual Leadership: Moving People on to God's Agenda.* Nashville, TN: Broadman and Holman Publishers, 2001.

Blanchard, Ken, John P. Carlos, and Alan Randolph. *Empowerment Takes More Than a Minute.* New York: MJF Books, 1996.

_____. *The 3 Keys to Empowerment: Release the Power Within People for Astonishing Results.* San Francisco: Berrett-Koehler Publishers, 1999.

Borden, Paul D. *Hitting the Bullseye: How Denominations Can Aim the Congregation at the Mission Field.* Nashville: Abingdon Press, 2003.

Brown, Daniel A. *The Other Side of Pastoral Ministry: Using Process Leadership to Transform Your Church.* Grand Rapids: Zondervan, 1996.

Campbell, Clifton P. "Peer Training and Teamwork: Industry Trend or Event." Providence Business News, August 16, 1999 v14 i18 p38. Available from http://web6.infotrac.galegroup.com/itw/infomark/ 263/75/33717380w6/purl=rc1_EAIM_0_ A55900675&dyn=3!xrn_1_0_A55900675?sw_ aep=spri52628. Accessed 27 March 2003.

Campbell, LeAnn. "Finding (and Keeping) Happy Volunteers: Don't Loose Your Volunteers to Burnout." Available from http://www.christianitytoday.com/ bcl/areas/teamdevelopment/articles/092904.html. Accessed 8 August 2004.

Cedar, Paul A. *Strength in Servant Leadership.* Waco, Texas: Word Books Publishers, 1987.

Cladis, George. *Leading the Team-Based Church: How Pastors and Church Staffs Can Grow Together Into a Powerful Fellowship of Leaders.* San Francisco: Jossey-Bass Publishers, 1999.

Clinton, J. Robert. *Leadership Emergence Theory: A Self-Study Manual for Analyzing the Development of a Christian Leader.* Altadena, CA: Dr. Bobby Clinton, 1989.

Collins, Jim *Good to Great: Why Some Companies Make the Leap...and Others Don't.* New York: HarperBusiness, 2001.

Cordeiro, Wayne. *Doing Church as a Team.* Ventura, California: Regal Books, 2001.

Dresselhaus, Richard L. "Passing the Torch: The Art of Mentoring Staff." *Enrichment: A Journal for Pentecostal Ministry* (Winter 2003): 66-70.

_____. "The Long Reach of Laity." *Enrichment: A Journal for Pentecostal Ministry* (Fall 1998): 57.

"Effective Churches and Team Leadership," *Next,* vol. 5, no. 2 (April, May, June 1999), [journal on-line]. Available from http://www.leadnet.org/archives/NEXT/apr99.pdf. Accessed 10 October 2002.

Elliston, Edgar J. *Home Grown Leaders.* Pasadena, California: William Carey Library, 1992.

Elmore, Tim. *Mentoring: How to Invest Your Life in Others.* Duluth, GA: EQUIP, 2001.

Enrichment Editors. "Empowering Believers for Service: Interview with Ronald McManus, Jerry Strandquist, Bill Hull." *Enrichment: A Journal for Pentecostal Ministry* (Winter 1997): 14-19.

Eskelin, Neil. *Leading with Love: and Getting More Results.* Grand Rapids: Fleming H. Revell, 2001.

Ford, Leighton. *Transforming Leadership: Jesus' Way of Creating Vision, Shaping Values, and Empowering Change.* Downers Grove: InterVarsity Press, 1991.

George, Carl F. *The Coming Church Revolution: Empowering Leaders for the Future.* Grand Rapids: Fleming H. Revell, 1994.

Gibbs, Eddie. *ChurchNext: Quantum Changes in How We Do Ministry.* Downers Grove, Illinois: InterVarsity Press, 2000.

Haggard, Ted. *Dog Training, Fly Fishing, & Sharing Christ in the 21st Century: Empowering Your Church to Build Community Through Shared Interests.* Nashville: Thomas Nelson Publishers, 2002.

Hayes, Clancy P. "Training: The Secret of Pastoral Success." *Enrichment: A Journal for Pentecostal Ministry* (Fall 2002): 61.

Herrington, Jim, Mike Bonem, and James H. Furr. *Leading Congregational Change: A Practical Guide to the Transformational Journey.* San Francisco: Jossey-Bass, 2000.

Hodges, Melvin J. *The Indigenous Church: A Complete Handbook on How to Grow Young Churches.* Springfield, MO: Gospel Publishing House, 1976.

Hybels, Bill. *Courageous Leadership.* Grand Rapids: Zondervan, 2002.

_____. "The Y Factor: In Tough Times, You Need to Radically Increase Your Ministry's Volunteer Quotient." *Leadership: A Practical Journal for Church Leaders* 24, no. 1 (winter 2003): 78.

Knoth, Rick. "Children's Ministries – Building Tomorrow's Church: Interview with David Boyd, Dick Gruber, and Jim Wideman." *Enrichment: A Journal for Pentecostal Ministry* (Summer 2001): 10.

Macchia, Stephen A. *Becoming A Healthy Church: 10 Characteristics.* Grand Rapids: Baker Books, 1999.

Mallory, Sue and Brad Smith. *The Equipping Church Guidebook.* Grand Rapids: Zondervan, 2001.

Marshall, Tom. *Understanding Leadership: Fresh Perspectives on the Essentials of New Testament Leadership.* Lynnwood, Washington: Emerald Books, 1991.

Martz, David. *Leadership Development Architecture: Growing 21st Century Leaders in Cross-Cultural Bible Schools.* Springfield, Missouri: LIFE Publishers International, 2002.

Maxwell, John C. *Developing the Leaders Around You: How to Help Others Reach Their Full Potential.* Nashville: Thomas Nelson Publishers, 1995.

_____. "The Call to Equip: The Answer to Ministry Growth." *Enrichment: A Journal for Pentecostal Ministry* (Spring 2002): 61-65.

McIntosh, Gary L. "Empowering a New Culture of Service in Your Church." *Enrichment: A Journal for Pentecostal Ministry* (Fall 1998): 37.

McKenna, David L. *Power to Follow, Grace to Lead: Strategy for the Future of Christian Leadership.* Dallas: Word Publishing. 1989.

McLaren, Brian D. *The Church on the Other Side: Doing Ministry in the Postmodern Matrix.* Grand Rapids: Zondervan, 2000.

Milavec, Aaron. *To Empower as Jesus Did: Acquiring Spiritual Power Through Apprenticeship.* Toronto Studies in Theology: vol. 9. New York: The Edwin Mellen Press, 1982.

Moore, Steve. *Leadership Insights: For Emerging Leaders and Those Investing in Them.* Fort Worth: Top Flight Leadership, 2002.

Mundey, Paul. *Unlocking Church Doors: The Keys to Positive Change.* Leadership Insight Series, ed. Herb Miller. Nashville: Abingdon Press, 1997.

Northouse, Peter G. *Leadership: Theory and Practice*, 2^d ed. Thousand Oaks: Sage Publications, 2001.

Osei-Mensah, Gottfried. *Wanted: Servant Leaders.* Ghana, West Africa: Africa Christian Press, 1990.

Ott, Stanley E. *Twelve Dynamic Shifts for Transforming Your Church.* Grand Rapids: William B. Eerdmans, 2002.

Pasternack, Bruce A. and Albert J. Viscio. *The Centerless Corporation: A New Model for Transforming Your Organization for Growth and Prosperity.* New York: Simon & Schuster, 1998.

Petersen, Jim. Church *Without Walls: Moving Beyond Traditional Boundaries.* Colorado Springs, Colorado: Navpress, 1992.

Rector , Kristi. "Lessons from the Leaders." *Vital Ministry: Innovative and Practical Ideas for Pastors* (May/ June 1999): 64-67.

_____. "Power to the People – How Pastors can Empower their Congregations to be Lay Pastors: An Interview with Melvin Steinbron." *Vital Ministry: Innovative and Practical Ideas for Pastors* (July/August 1998): 44-45.

Reed, Bobbie and John Westfall. *Building Strong People: How to Lead Effectively.* Grand Rapids: Baker Books, 1997.

Reid, Tommy. "A Spiritual Father's Reflection on Mentoring: Confessions of a Spiritual Father." *Enrichment: A Journal for Pentecostal Ministry* (Summer 1997): 48-51.

Schaller, Lyle E. *The Small Church is Different!* Nashville: Abingdon Press, 1982.

Schwarz, Christian. *The ABC's of Natural Church Development.* Carol Stream, Illinois: ChurchSmart Resources, 1998.

Shawchuck, Norman and Roger Heuser. *Leading the Congregation: Caring for Yourself While Serving the People.* Nashville: Abingdon Press, 1993.

_____. *Managing the Congregation: Building Effective Systems to Serve People.* Nashville: Abingdon Press, 1996.

Sherriton, Jacalyn and James L. Stern. *Corporate Culture/ Team Culture: Removing the Hidden Barriers to Team Success.* New York: AMACOM, 1997.

Sidebar. *Enrichment: A Journal for Pentecostal Ministry* (Spring 2002): 62.

Slaughter, Michael. *UnLearning Church.* Loveland, Colorado: Group Publishing, 2000.

Slocum, Robert E. *Maximize Your Ministry.* Colorado Springs: NavPress, 1990.

Spurling, John H. "Empowered Team Leaders in the Smaller Church." *Enrichment: A Journal for Pentecostal Ministry* (Fall 2001): 52-54.

Steinbron, Melvin J. *Can the Pastor Do It Alone?: A Model for Preparing Lay People for Lay Pastoring.* Ventura, California: Regal Books, 1987.

_____. *The Lay Driven Church: How to Empower the People in Your Church to Share the Tasks of Ministry.* Ventura, California: Regal Books, 1997.

Stevens, R. Paul and Phil Collins. *The Equipping Pastor.* Washington, D.C.: The Alban Institute, 1993. As quoted in Melvin J Steinbron, *The Lay Driven Church: How to Empower the People in Your Church to Share the Tasks of Ministry.* Ventura, California: Regal Books, 1997.

Tichy, Noel M. *The Leadership Engine: How Winning Companies Build Leaders at Every Level.* New York: HarperBusiness, 1997.

Warden, Michael D. "Generational Trends." *Vital Ministry: Innovative and Practical Ideas for Pastors* (November/December 1997): 50-54.

Warren, Rick. *The Purpose Driven Church: Growth Without Compromising Your Message and Mission.* Grand Rapids: Zondervan, 1995.

Warren, Rick, "Who's On First?: Guiding Your Members into Greater Maturity." *Enrichment: A Journal for Pentecostal Ministry* (Summer 2002): 56.

Wheatley, Margaret. "Goodbye, Command and Control." *Leader to Leader,* No. 5 Summer 1997. Available from http://drucker.org/leaderbooks/L2L/summer97/wheatley.html. Accessed 6 October 2004.

White, James Emery. *Rethinking the Church: A Challenge to Creative Redesign in an Act of Transition.* Grand Rapids: Baker Books, 1997.

Wilkes, Gene C. *Jesus on Leadership: Discovering the Secrets of Servant Leadership from the Life of Christ.* Wheaton, Illinois: Tyndale, 1998.

Young, Howard. "Rediscovering Servant Leadership." *Enrichment: A Journal for Pentecostal Ministry* (Spring 2002): 34.

Empowerment and Biblical Theology

Barrett, Lois, Inagrace T. Dietterich, George R. Hunsberger, Alan J. Roxburgh, and Craig Van Gelder. *Missional Church: A Vision for the Sending of the Church in North America,* ed. D.L. Guder. Grand Rapids: William B. Eerdmans, 1998.

Foulkes, Francis. *The Epistle of Paul to the Ephesians: An Introduction and Commentary.* Tyndale New Testament Commentaries. Grand Rapids: William B. Eerdmans, 1963.

Gaebelein, Frank E. ed. *The Expositor's Bible Commentary: with the New International Version of the Holy Bible, vol. 11, Ephesians – Philemon,* by A. Skevington Wood. Grand Rapids: Zondervan, 1978.

Guder, Darrell L. *The Continuing Conversion of the Church.* Grand Rapids: William B. Eerdmans, 2000.

Harris, R. Laird ed. *Theological Wordbook of the Old Testament,* vol. 1. Chicago: Moody Press, 1980.

Hildebrandt, Wilf. *An Old Testament Theology of the Spirit of God.* Peabody, Massachusetts: Hendrickson Publishers, 1995.

Kaiser, Walter C. *Toward an Old Testament Theology.* Grand Rapids: Zondervan, 1978.

Kittel, Gerhard ed. *Theological Dictionary of the New Testament*, vol. 1. Grand Rapids: William B. Eerdmans, 1964.

_____. *Theological Dictionary of the New Testament*, vol. 2. Grand Rapids: William B. Eerdmans, 1964.

Lasor, William Sanford, David Allan Hubbard, and Frederic Wm. Bush. *Old Testament Survey: The Message, Form, and Background of the Old Testament.* Grand Rapids: William B. Eerdmans, 1982.

Lenski, R.C.H. *The Interpretation of St. Paul's Epistles to the Galatians, to the Ephesians, and to the Philippians.* Minneapolis, MN: Augsburg Publishing House, 1937.

Martens, Elmer A. *God's Design: A Focus on Old Testament Theology.* Grand Rapids: Baker Books, 1994.

Peters, George W. *A Biblical Theology of Missions.* Chicago: Moody Press, 1972.

Reyburn, William D. and Euan McG. Fry. A Handbook on Genesis. UBS Handbook Series. New York: United Bible Societies, 1997.

Reymond, R. L. "Offices of Christ," in *Evangelical Dictionary of Theology*, ed. Walter A. Elwell. Grand Rapids: Baker Book House, 1984.

Richards, Lawrence O. and Gib Martin. *A Theology of Personal Ministry: Spiritual Giftedness in the Local Church*. Grand Rapids: Zondervan, 1981.

Stronstad, Roger. *The Charismatic Theology of St. Luke*. Peabody, Massachusetts: Hendrickson Publishers, 1984.